Excel

Basic Skills

Writing Skills

3–4 Years

Ages 8-10

Get the Results You Want!

N Colvin

PASCAL PRESS

Reprinted 2001, 2002, 2004, 2006, 2007, 2008, 2009, 2010, 2012

Updated in 2013 for the Australian Curriculum

Reprinted 2014, 2016, 2017 (twice), 2020, 2021, 2022, 2024

ISBN 978 1 74020 046 2

Pascal Press
PO Box 250
Glebe NSW 2037
(02) 9198 1748
www.pascalpress.com.au

Publisher: Vivienne Joannou
Edited by Shelley Barons and Rosemary Peers
Text design and typesetting by Tarnie Lowson
Additional typesetting by Grizzly Graphics (Leanne Richters)
Cover by DiZign Pty Ltd
Printed by Vivar Printing/Green Giant Press

Contents

Introduction

This book is designed to help Year 3 and Year 4 students develop and increase their creative writing skills. It is a clear and practical guide to writing well-structured, grammatically correct English. The book is divided into units based on various narrative and non-fiction types of texts. Each unit provides a model text, followed by a variety of practical exercises that cover the important grammar, vocabulary and punctuation points to be learned when writing for that specific type of text. Answers are provided in a convenient lift-out section in the centre.

Unit 1: Narrative

Narrative texts tell a story.

Strike Me Pink!

Because we lived near the beach, our cousins visited one Easter. Unfortunately it rained all weekend. Just imagine eight children under ten years old and four adults cooped up in one tiny cottage. Everyone's patience was wearing thin. We children were starting to whinge and niggle each other. The adults were trying to keep cool and prevent us from hurting each other.

One night when it was all too much, the children were sent to bed early. Four of us were on mattresses on the floor. The line for drying washing, strung across the room overhead, held only one item: my pink dressing gown. I had carelessly tossed it there out of the way.

When Dad came in for a goodnight kiss he thought we looked like a row of toy soldiers in a box. Bending down he exclaimed, "Strike me pink!" And he was! The dressing gown fell from the line and draped over his shoulders like a cloak. What mirth erupted at the sight of my father looking like a pink general. The tensions eased and smiles returned to everyone's faces.

The next morning was fine as our cousins left for home. We hadn't been to the beach, but we did have a story to share that would bring a smile to our faces for many years to come.

Expressive Verbs

show thoughts and feelings, as well as actions

imagine
whinge
niggle
keep cool
exclaimed

Nouns

name people, places and things

cousins
beach
children
mattresses
line

Adjectives

possessive adjectives tell to whom things belong

our
everyone's
my
his

☆ ☆ ☆ ☆

Did you notice these important types of words in the narrative above? Read the story again and find the verbs, nouns and adjectives.

Some doing verbs help to show what the characters are thinking and feeling.
e.g. *We children were starting to* ***niggle*** *each other.*
Other doing verbs we could use are *annoy*, *pester*, *bother*.

1 Use other doing, feeling and saying words to complete these sentences.

a We children were starting to whinge.

We children were starting to ___________.

b The adults were trying to keep cool and prevent us from hurting each other.

The adults were trying to ___________ and prevent us from hurting each other.

c Bending down Dad exclaimed, "Strike me pink!"

Bending down Dad ___________, "Strike me pink!"

Nouns are names of people, places and things. They are used to identify people, places and things in the story.
e.g. *Eight* ***children*** *and four* ***adults*** *were cooped up in one tiny* ***cottage****.*
Synonyms are words that have the same meaning. They could be used instead and not change the meaning of the sentence.
Synonyms that could be used for **cottage** are *house*, *home*, *cabin*, *shack*.

2 Use noun synonyms to complete these sentences. Try to think of at least two different words.

a Because we lived near the beach, our cousins visited one Easter.

Because we lived near the ___________, our cousins visited one Easter.

Because we lived near the ___________, our cousins visited one Easter.

b The adults were trying to keep cool.

The ___________ were trying to keep cool.

The ___________ were trying to keep cool.

c We hadn't been to the beach, but we did have a story to share.

We hadn't been to the beach, but we did have a ___________ to share.

We hadn't been to the beach, but we did have a ___________ to share.

d What mirth erupted at the sight of my father.

What ___________ erupted at the sight of my father.

What ___________ erupted at the sight of my father.

Sometimes writers provide more information about the nouns by using adjectives to describe them.

e.g. *my **pink** dressing gown*

3 **Write suitable adjectives that could be used to add information about these nouns.**

the beach	eight children
one night	on mattresses
a smile	a story

Possessive adjectives are used to show possession or who owns something.

e.g. ***My** pink dressing gown* tells that the dressing gown belongs to ***me***.

4 **In the following sentences underline the possessive adjective and write a noun to show who the thing belongs to.**

a Because we lived near the beach, our cousins visited one Easter.

b The dressing gown draped over his shoulders.

c Everyone's patience was wearing thin.

5 **Write the correct possessive adjectives to complete each sentence.**

a The young boy was very pleased to see new boogie board.

b You need to apply sunscreen to skin before going out into the sun.

c Our cousins came to visit us in new car.

Direct speech means the actual words that somebody says. Speech marks are used to show the words that are said.

e.g. *"Strike me pink!" exclaimed Dad.*
"You look like a pink general," I said.

6 **Use speech marks to show which words the people actually say.**

a I wish we could go outside and play, said Anne.

You will be able to go out when it stops raining, replied Mum.

But I don't think it will ever stop raining, sighed Jason, looking at the heavy grey clouds. It's been raining for days and days.

b Write two sentences to show what you think may have been said after the conversation above. Don't forget to use speech marks to show which words are actually spoken.

7 Picture Study

Use nouns to label all the different things you can see in the picture.

Choose four of those nouns. Write a sentence to tell about each one. Include action verbs.

a

b

c ______________________________

____

d ______________________________

____

8 Words to Tell About Feelings

The writer has told us how the characters are feeling without actually using feeling words. Re-read the story. Think about how the characters would be feeling and what words tell you that. Write what you know below.

a At the beginning, the children were feeling because

____

b At the beginning, the adults were feeling because

____

c Dad was feeling because

____

d At the end, everyone was feeling because

____

9 Picture Strip

The four pictures below tell a story in sequence. Look at them carefully. Clues about the characters and the setting (where the story takes place) are given below the pictures. Use the pictures and the clues to make up your own story. Write two interesting sentences about each picture. Try to use some direct speech to tell what the characters are saying.

Mark, Samantha and Spike at Forest Park

____

____

10 Proofreading

Where do the capital letters and full stops go? Mark them.

the children were inside the house they were waiting for the sun to come out they wanted to go outside and play they were getting bored and were starting to fight their parents were beginning to feel annoyed soon the sun came out and they were able to go out and play then everyone was happy again

Unit 2: Recount

Recounts tell events in sequence. Diary entries are one type of recount.

The Day I Broke My Arm

Dear Diary,

Today began just like normal, but it didn't finish that way. It was the last day of term and I couldn't wait to go to the beach tomorrow. School was okay, but after school I had gymnastics. I always enjoy gym, but it's really great on the last day because we play games.

Gym was fun—at first! Then we played volleyball, and that's when it happened. While I was running backwards to hit the ball, I tripped over a tricycle that another child was riding. He couldn't get out of the way quickly enough.

I fell and landed right on my shoulder. Ow! Did it hurt! The coach rushed over and asked if I could wriggle my fingers. I couldn't, so she thought my shoulder was probably dislocated. She immediately phoned Mum and Dad. It didn't take long for them to come and take me to Emergency at the hospital.

I cried all the way. Luckily we saw a doctor fairly soon and a morphine injection helped stop the pain. After that some X-rays showed that my arm (my humerus) was broken. Fortunately the fracture's not bad and I only have to wear a sling. The weight of my elbow will help to straighten my arm, but I won't be able to do gym, or swimming or any sports for at least six weeks.

I'm still looking forward to my holiday tomorrow, but it won't be quite the same.

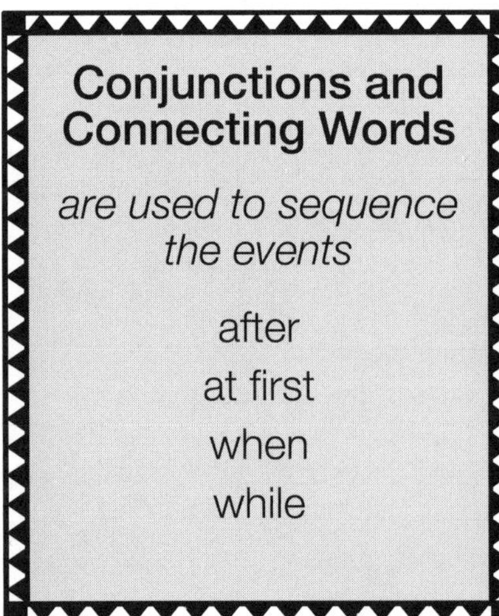

Conjunctions and Connecting Words

are used to sequence the events

after
at first
when
while

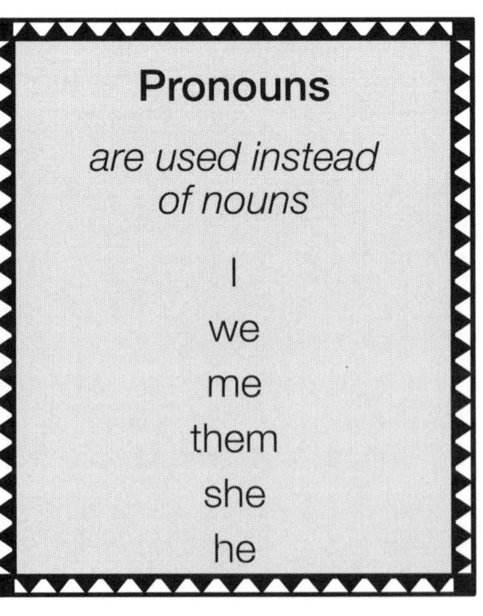

Pronouns

are used instead of nouns

I
we
me
them
she
he

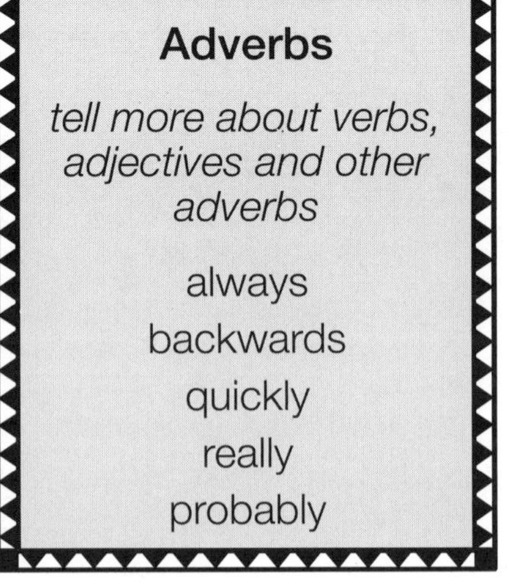

Adverbs

tell more about verbs, adjectives and other adverbs

always
backwards
quickly
really
probably

☆ ☆ ☆ ☆

Did you notice these important types of words in the recount above?
Read the diary entry again and find the conjunctions, pronouns and adverbs.

Connecting words are used to show when the events occurred and in what sequence.
e.g. ***After*** *school I had gymnastics*.
Other time words which could be used to tell a different time are *when*, *before*, *during*.

1 Use these time words to complete the sentences and show the sequence.

when, after that, at first, after, while

One day school, it was very hot, we decided to go for a swim. The water felt cold but we were soon having fun and didn't notice it. Some friends came to visit we were swimming. They came in for a swim too. we all got out and played on the grass.

Pronouns are words that can be used instead of nouns. Nouns are the names of people, places and things. The correct pronoun must be used for the nouns they represent.
e.g. *The coach is a woman.* ***She*** *phoned Mum and Dad.*

2 Use the correct pronoun to complete the following sentences.

I, she, he, me, them

a When Coach Kate looked at my arm thought it was dislocated.

b My parents came to take me to the hospital because was hurt.

c The doctor I saw was John Knox. told me that my arm was broken.

d My parents were pleased that my coach had called .

e The doctor showed how to keep my arm in a sling.

Adverbs tell more about verbs. They tell how, when and where something happened.
e.g. *I* ***always*** *enjoy gym* tells **when** I enjoy gym.
Other adverbs that could be used are *sometimes*, *often*, *usually*, *never*.

3 Use other adverbs to complete these sentences to tell how or when something happened.

a I was running **backwards** to hit the ball.

I was running to hit the ball.

b The coach immediately phoned my parents.

The coach phoned my parents.

c The coach came over quickly to see what happened.

The coach came over to see what happened.

> Sometimes adverbs are used to give more meaning to adjectives and other adverbs.
> e.g. *Gym is **really** great on the last day* tells **how great** gym is.

4 Use other adverbs to complete these sentences to give more information about these adjectives and adverbs.

a The coach thought that my shoulder was probably dislocated.

The coach thought that my shoulder was dislocated.

b We saw the doctor fairly soon.

We saw the doctor soon.

c The fracture is not bad.

The fracture is bad.

5 Use a different adverb to complete each sentence.

a My gym coach was helpful.

b The boy on the tricycle was moving slowly.

c I could wait for the holidays that started the next day.

6 Sequencing Sentences

The following sentences are not in the correct order.

- ☆ **Read them carefully.**
- ☆ **Underline the words that help you understand the sequence.**
- ☆ **Number the sentences to show the order in which they happened.**
- ☆ **Write one more sentence to complete the sequence.**
- ☆ **Begin that sentence with the word *After*.**

_____ Samantha went next.

_____ Before they left, they had to get all their gear together.

_____ Bruce was first to have a turn.

_____ Then they walked to the ramp.

_____ Last of all Peter had a turn.

_____ The children decided to go rollerblading at the ramp.

____

Exclamation marks are used to show strong feelings like excitement, anger, surprise, or hurt.

e.g. *Gym was fun—at first!*
Ow! Did it hurt!

7 **Use exclamation marks to show surprise and excitement in the following recount. Write a sentence to end the recount.**

I was lying on my bed thinking about what to do. Suddenly—*rinnng*. It was the doorbell.

"Who could that be?" I wondered.

I rushed to the door and opened it.

"Surprise," exclaimed Dad.

I couldn't see any surprise at first. I was puzzled. Then Dad brought something out from behind his back. A dog.

____

____

8 **A skeleton outline of a story is made up of some of the main words in each sentence. To complete the story you must write out each sentence so that it makes sense. Make sure you use connecting words to sequence your story, and adverbs to give more meaning to the verbs, adjectives and other adverbs.**

A Farm Holiday

a Jessie, Sam going grandparents farm holiday.

____

____

b excited never holiday on own

____

____

c first day fed chickens grain scraps collected eggs

____

____

d picnic lunch riverbank catch guppies jar

____

____

e last grandfather took ride horse paddock tractor

9 Picture Strip

The four pictures below tell the events of one day. Look at them carefully. The clocks in the corners show the sequence of events. Write two sentences about each picture to give a recount of the day's events. Use time words to connect the sentences. Try to use adverbs to make your recount more interesting.

10 Proofreading

Put in the missing capital letters and full stops. There is a place for one exclamation mark also.

the children were visiting their grandparents for the holidays and they were really enjoying it they had never been to sydney before and everything looked so big and imposing suddenly they turned a corner and they saw the harbour bridge wow the children had never seen such an enormous bridge before

Unit 3: Information Report

Information Reports provide information about a particular thing.

The Didgeridoo

The didgeridoo is the traditional musical instrument of the Aboriginal people of Australia. It has been used for hundreds of years to accompany their traditional dances and ceremonies.

A didgeridoo is made from a living tree trunk that has been hollowed out by termites. The size and the shape of the hole determine the sound made by the instrument, so choosing the right tree can be a difficult task.

When a suitable tree has been found, it is cut down and left to dry. Then the bark is removed. Sometimes the log may be shaped or hollowed further to give the desired sound.

Most didgeridoos are between 1 and 2 metres in length with the mouthpiece at the narrow end. Many didgeridoos are decorated with paintings of traditional designs.

The didgeridoo is played by using a special type of breathing. The player breathes in through his nose. At the same time he breathes out into the mouthpiece through his mouth. This helps him to maintain the continuous sound for as long as desired.

Relating Verbs

provide information

is

are

was

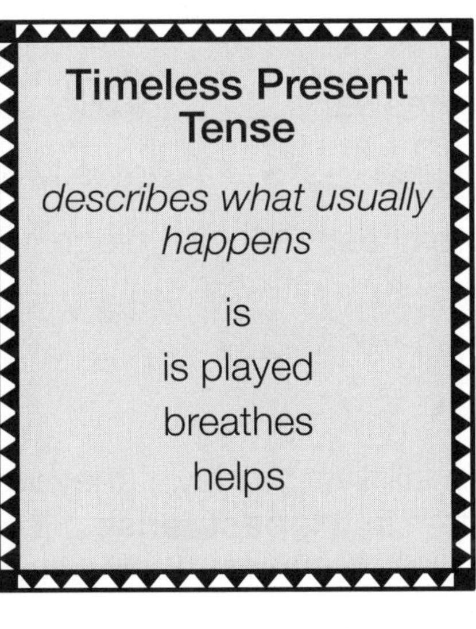

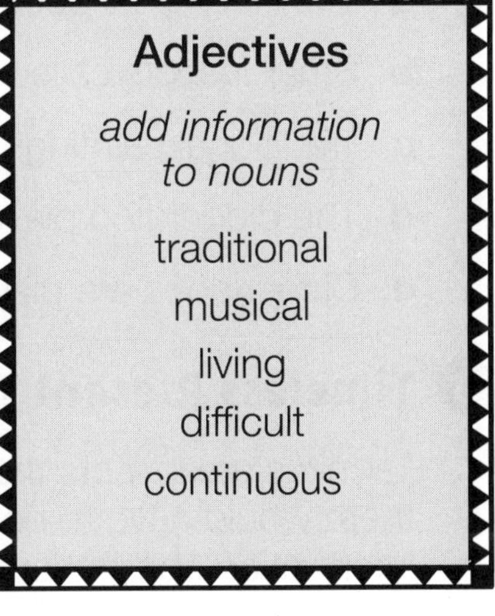

☆ ☆ ☆ ☆

Did you notice these important types of words in the information report above?

Read it again and find the relating verbs, present-tense verbs and adjectives.

Relating verbs are used to provide more information about a noun.

e.g. *A didgeridoo* ***is*** *made from a living tree trunk.* (one)

Most didgeridoos ***are*** *between 1 and 2 metres in length.* (more than one)

1 Choose the correct relating verb to complete these sentences.

a A didgeridoo __________ used in traditional dances and ceremonies. (is, are)

b Different colours of paint __________ used to decorate the outside of didgeridoos. (is, are)

c The mouthpiece __________ at the narrow end of the didgeridoo. (is, are)

d Termites __________ insects that eat mainly wood. (is, are)

e Suitable trees __________ ones with hollow trunks. (is, are)

The timeless present tense tells what is usual. The action described is continuous.

e.g. *The size and the shape of the hole* ***determine*** *the sound made by the instrument.*

2 The following sentences use timeless present tense to tell what is usual, but the sentence beginnings and endings are mixed up. Draw lines to connect the sentences correctly.

a The Aboriginal people of Australia play	in and out at the same time.
b Small insects called termites eat	to decorate didgeridoos.
c Traditional paintings are used	mostly by men.
d The didgeridoo player breathes	didgeridoos to dance to.
e Didgeridoos are played	the wood of trees.

3 Timeless Present Tense

Termites are insects that are still living today. If they were extinct, information about them would have to be written in the **past tense**. However, since they still exist, information about them must be written in the **timeless present tense**.

☆ Read the following information about termites.

☆ Underline the words written in past tense.

☆ On the lines below, rewrite the information about termites using timeless present tense.

Termites were insects that lived in many parts of the world. Like all other insects, termites had three body parts and six legs. Although termites were often called 'white ants' they were not ants. Termites lived in large colonies. Each colony had at least one king and queen. Only the king and queen termites had wings. Queen termites could lay more than 1000 eggs a day. Most termites ate wood, bark, leaves and other parts of trees.

Adjectives are used to describe or add information about a noun or a noun group. They help us to make a more detailed and interesting mental picture of the noun being described.

e.g. *A didgeridoo is made from a* ***living*** *tree trunk.*

4 **Re-read the Information Report about the didgeridoo. Look for other adjectives used to describe it. Write them on the lines below.**

5 **Use two suitable adjectives to complete each sentence.**

a The dinosaur stampeded across the field.

b The mosquito bit the weary traveller.

c The motorbike roared along the track.

d The fly was eaten by the frog.

6 **Timeless present tense is used when talking or writing about a situation that is usual or continuous. Use the following words to write sentences about the Simpson Desert. Write them in timeless present tense.**

Simpson Desert

a Simpson Desert   situated   central Australia

____

____

b sand ridge desert   red   sand dunes   north to south

____

____

c temperature   hot   day   cool   night

____

____

d arid   rainfall   less than 250 mm   annually

____

____

e animals   hundreds   birds   reptiles   mammals

____

____

Commas are used to separate items in a list.

e.g. *Most termites eat wood, bark, leaves and other parts of trees.*

In this list the last item of food is *parts of trees*. It is preceded by *and*. No comma is needed when *and* is used.

7 **Put the commas in the correct places in these lists. Then write one list of your own using commas to separate the different items.**

a Many different animals live in deserts including bandicoots bilbies euros goannas thorny devils and wedge-tailed eagles.

b When I go to the beach I always take my hat t-shirt sunscreen boogie board bucket and spade.

c There are five people in my family. They are Mum Dad Paul Joanna and me.

d ____

____

8 Picture Study

Look at this picture of a snakes and ladders board. Use the labels and information in the picture to write four sentences describing the board. Make sure to use relating verbs and timeless present tense. Try to use some adjectives if possible.

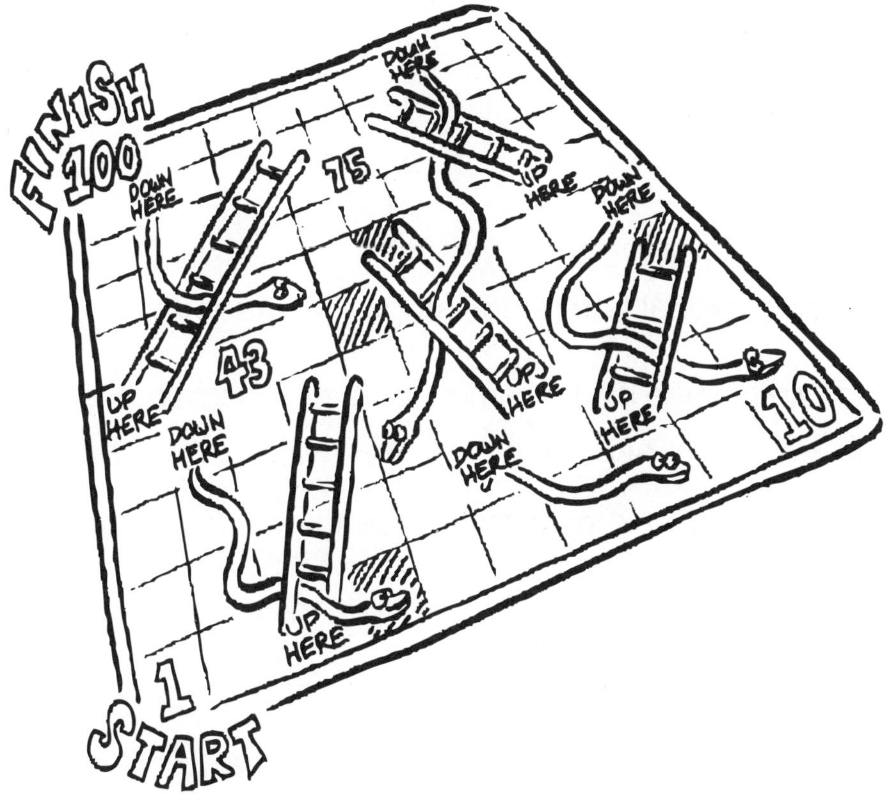

a ____

____

b ____

____

c ____

____

d ____

____

9 Sentence Building

Build new sentences using the first sentences as models.

a A didgeridoo is made from a living tree trunk that has been hollowed out by termites.

A is made from that has been

.

b The didgeridoo is played by using a special type of breathing.

The is played by .

c The didgeridoo has been used for hundreds of years to accompany traditional dances and ceremonies.

The has been used for to

.

10 Proofreading

Put in the missing capital letters, full stops and commas.

kelsey couldn't wait for the long summer holidays to begin her family was going on a four-wheel drive holiday to the simpson desert kelsey was looking forward to seeing the long red sand dunes spinifex grass wedge-tailed eagles thorny devils and bilbies

Review 1

1 Transforming Sentences

New sentences can be made simply by substituting words in one sentence for other words. Change the underlined words in each sentence to make two new sentences.

a The children were going to the beach.

The were going to the .

The were going to the .

b The little boy was riding the tricycle.

The was the .

The was the .

c The bilby has long rabbit-like ears and silky blue-grey fur.

The has ears and

fur.

The has ears and

fur.

2 Expanding Sentences

Adjectives and adverbs can make sentences more interesting and help to create a clearer mental picture.

e.g. *The grey-haired old man spoke kindly to the little lost dog.*
is more interesting and gives more information than *The man spoke to the dog.*

Add appropriate adjectives and adverbs to these sentences to make them more interesting.

a The car went down the road.

b The girl wore a hat to the beach.

c The child sat on the seat.

d The bilby stayed in the burrow.

3 Sequencing a Recount

The following five sentences give a recount of a boat trip, however, they are not in sequence. Write the numbers to show the correct order, then write a sixth sentence to complete the recount.

_____ After they had gone a short way from shore, they dropped anchor and put their lines in the clear blue water.

_____ Before anyone else could catch a fish, the skies darkened and a wind blew up.

_____ The day was fine when the family set out in their motorboat for a day's fishing.

_____ Then Paul felt a tug on his line but all he caught was a knotty eel.

_____ Sam was the first to feel a tug on her line and she reeled in a beautiful bream.

____

____

4 Picture Study

Use nouns to label all the different things you can see in the picture.

Choose four of those nouns. List them here. Write two adjectives to describe each noun.

Nouns **Adjectives**

a

b

c

d

Now write a sentence about each of those nouns using the adjectives.

a ____

____

b ____

____

c ____

____

d ____

____

5 Punctuation

a Speech marks are used to show the exact words that somebody says. Put the speech marks in the correct places in the following sentences. Then write a third sentence to complete the conversation.

Look at that, said Mary.
What is it? asked Dan.

____

____

b Exclamation marks are used to show strong feelings, like excitement or surprise. Put the exclamation marks in appropriate places in the following sentences.

Ben and Jade were looking for tiny creatures in the backyard. Suddenly they heard a strange sound.
"Ssh " whispered Ben. "Did you hear that?"
"Yes," replied Jade, also whispering. "What do you think it was?"
Then Jade tugged at Ben's arm. "Oh look " she said, and she pointed into the lower branches of the flowering bottlebrush.
"Where?" asked Ben.
"There " said Jade, watching the tiny birds cheeping for their food.
"Wow " said Ben when he realised what Jade had seen.

c Commas are used to separate items in a list. Put commas in the correct places in the list. Then write a list of your favourite foods.

When I go to camp I need to take my sleeping bag pillow pyjamas toothbrush comb two pairs of shoes and lots of warm clothes.

My favourite foods are ____

____

____.

Unit 4: Recount

Recounts tell events in sequence; they include factual and historical recounts.

Constructing a Worm Farm

In the school holidays my grandma came to stay. She is a keen gardener and helped me set up a worm farm for our garden.

On the very first morning we went to the hardware store. We bought some big black plastic containers designed especially for worm farms, a box of worms and some bedding material.

As soon as we arrived home, we got started. First we chose the location: a shady spot under the back pergola where it would stay cool and dry.

Next we organised the base. We put in some bedding material and moistened it before putting in the worms. We gave them just a little food at first: a few lettuce leaves, a bit of banana, an apple core and a few old blueberries. We put some wet newspapers on top and then put on the lid.

Every few days we gave the worms some fruit and vegetable scraps. They liked it all, even eggshells and tea leaves. But we did not give them meat, oranges or onions because worms don't like them much.

Soon we will have worm liquid to put on our garden, and worm castings in about four months. I love our worm farm. It is great for our garden and helps us reduce our waste!

Past-tense Verbs

places events in the past

came
helped
went
bought
gave

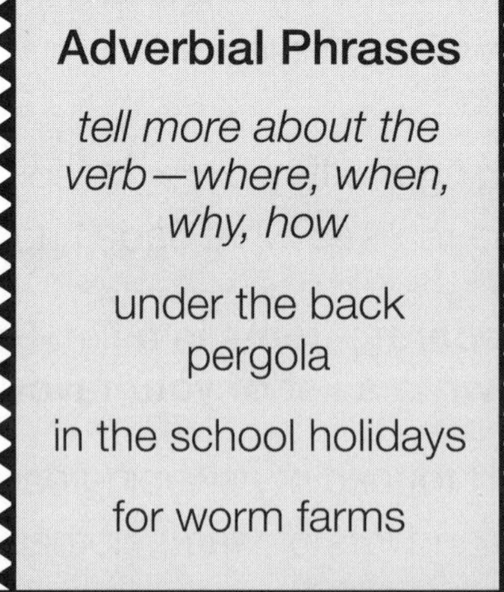

Adverbial Phrases

tell more about the verb—where, when, why, how

under the back pergola
in the school holidays
for worm farms

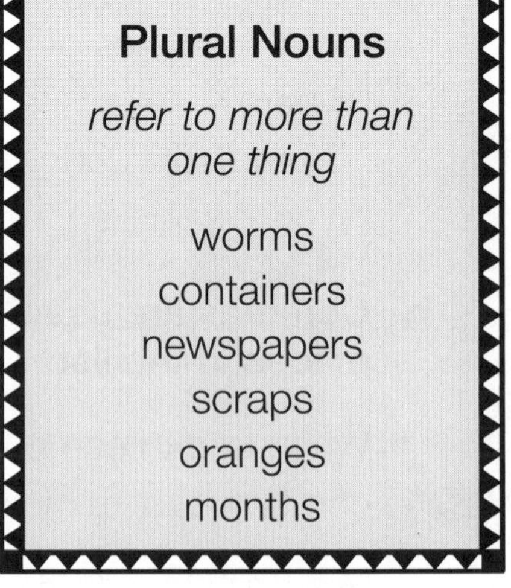

Plural Nouns

refer to more than one thing

worms
containers
newspapers
scraps
oranges
months

☆ ☆ ☆ ☆

Did you notice these important things in the recount above?
Read it again and find the past-tense verbs, adverbial phrases and plural nouns.

The past tense is used to tell about things that have already taken place.

Most verbs have *ed* added to the end for the past tense.

e.g. *Today I **help**. Yesterday I **helped**.*

When verbs end with *e*, only a *d* is added.

e.g. *Today I **arrive**. Yesterday I **arrived**.*

Some verbs change their spelling for the past tense.

e.g. *Today I **come**. Yesterday I **came**.*

The spelling of some verbs stays the same for both the past and present tense.

e.g. *Today I **spread**. Yesterday I **spread**.*

1 Write the following verbs in the past tense.

a Today I **live** in Australia. Last year I ___________ in England.

b Today I **tell** you what we will do. Yesterday I ___________ you what happened.

c Today Peter **suggests** that we go to the library. Yesterday Jessie ___________ we go to the movies.

d Today we **organise** scraps to feed the worms. Last week we ___________ the base of the worm farm.

e Now I **spread** peanut butter on my toast. Yesterday I ___________ honey on my toast.

A phrase is a group of words that has no verb.

Adverbial phrases give more information about verbs. They tell how, when, where or why things happen. There are two adverbial phrases in the following sentence.

e.g. ***On the very first morning** we went **to the hardware store**.*

On the very first morning tells when we went.

to the hardware store tells where we went.

2 Read the following sentences. The adverbial phrases are in bold type. Replace the adverbial phrase with another adverbial phrase. Make sure that the sentence still makes sense.

a **In the school holidays** my grandma came to stay.

____

____

b We put in some bedding material and moistened it **before putting in the worms**.

____

____

c Grandma helped me set up a worm farm **for our garden** in our backyard.

Plural nouns are used to refer to more than one thing.
Most often an *s* is added to make a singular noun plural. e.g. *worm—worms*
Sometimes *es* is added. e.g. *box—boxes*
When words end with *y*, usually the *y* is changed to *i* and *es* is added.
e.g. *berry—berries*
The spelling of some nouns stays the same for both singular and plural.
e.g. *fruit—fruit*
The plural of some nouns is more irregular. e.g. *child—children, leaf—leaves*

3 Write the plural form of the following nouns.

a one farm many

b one blueberry many

c one apple many

d one dish many

e one fish many

f one onion many

4 Past Tense

The following sentences were written with the events in the future; they had not yet happened. Rewrite the sentences in the past tense as though the events had already taken place.

a My grandma will come to visit and she will help me make a worm farm.

b First we will find a suitable location for our worm farm.

c We will feed the worms nearly every day.

d The worms will help our garden to grow.

5. **Underline the verb in these sentences. Add an adverbial phrase to give more information about the verb.**

a During the school holidays my grandma came to stay (how long)

____

b We went to the hardware store (when)

____

c We went to the hardware store (why)

____

d We set up the worm farm (where)

____

6. Picture Study

Complete these sentences. Write them in the past tense and include an adverbial phrase.

a The tyre ______________________________

____

b The girl ______________________________

____

c The boy ______________________________

____

d The dog ______________________________

____

7 Writing a Recount

The following notes were taken to write a recount. Only the main words for each sentence were written. To complete the recount you must write out each sentence in full so that it makes sense. Make sure to use the past tense, and use adverbial phrases where you can.

Coming to Australia

a great-great-grandfather ship from England 1864

____

____

b purchased land west of Sydney farming

____

____

c 1870 met Mary Cooper married soon

____

____

d one year later first child my great-grandfather born

____

____

e four children moved Sydney children school

____

____

8 Sequencing Sentences

The following five sentences are not in the correct sequence. Write numbers to show the order in which they occurred.

_____ Over the years they lovingly tended the tree and watched their children climb in it and play in its shade.

_____ Then they watered the seed and waited for it to grow.

_____ When the people moved into the house they decided to plant a tree.

_____ One day during a violent storm, after all the children had grown up, the tree was struck by lightning.

_____ First they chose the spot, dug the hole, and planted the seed.

Now write one more sentence to complete the recount.

9 More than One

Read the following sentences. They tell about one child. Rewrite the sentences so that they tell about more than one child. You will need to change some of the nouns, pronouns and verbs.

The young child sat on her seat waiting for her father. Today he was picking her up from school and taking her roller skating. The child already had her skates in her bag. As soon as she saw her father she jumped up and ran to him.

10 Proofreading

Read the following sentences. Some words are used incorrectly. Some words are misspelled. Make any corrections that are necessary. Put in the capital letters and full stops.

a my grandma go to the hardware store to bought some worm

b we find a cool and shady spot under the back pergolas

c last week we make the worms farm and give it some foods

d we gets worm liquids and castings to use on their gardens

Unit 5: Exposition

Expositions address questions and develop an argument.

Should Pet Cats Wear Bells?

The notion of fitting bells to domestic cats in order to reduce the harm they do to wildlife, especially birds, is popular at the moment, but not new. People have been doing so for hundreds of years. Although pet owners believe they are being responsible, bells are not effective in reducing the numbers of birds preyed upon by cats.

While a bell rings constantly with the cat's usual movement, as soon as the cat begins to stalk and prepares to pounce, the bell ceases to ring. The sudden movement of the pounce prevents the bell from ringing altogether due to the forces of inertia, and the bell does not sound again until impact occurs.

If a bell is not effective, what else can be done? While hunting is a natural instinct for cats, well-fed cats may be less likely to do so. De-sexing helps to ensure the cat population is manageable and, additionally, reduces the hunting drive. Finally, keeping cats inside at night guarantees they are not out hunting.

Although attaching a bell to a cat's collar may be better than doing nothing, there are more effective actions that can be taken. Responsible pet ownership is a positive step in the protection of wildlife.

Connecting Words

show contrasting ideas

but
although
while
if not ... what else

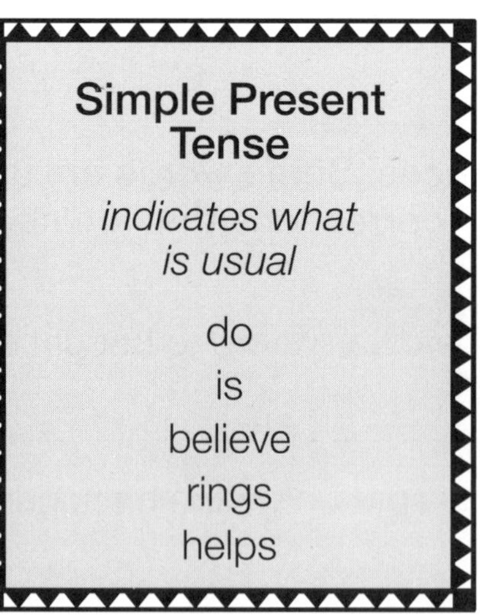

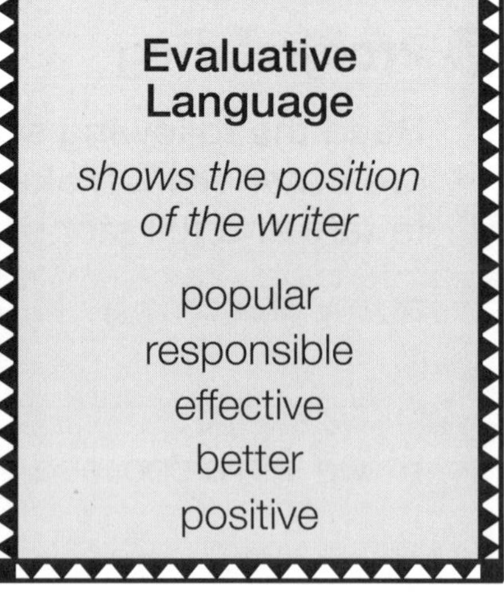

☆ ☆ ☆ ☆

Did you notice these important things in the exposition above?
Read it again and find the connecting words, simple present-tense words and any evaluative language.

Connecting words are used to show contrasting or differing ideas.

e.g. *The notion is popular* ***but*** *it is not new.*

Although *owners believe they are being responsible, bells are not effective.*

While *the bell rings as the cat moves, it stops ringing when the cat is about to pounce.*

1 Below are two sentences with contrasting ideas. Use a connecting word to combine them into one sentence.

a Hunting is a natural instinct for cats. Well-fed cats may be less likely to hunt.

___

b Cats like to hunt birds. Birds do not like to be caught by cats.

___

c People think they are being responsible by fitting bells. Bells are not really effective.

___

d A lot of people like to keep cats as pets. Some don't.

___

Simple present tense is used to indicate what is usual or continuous.

e.g. *Pet owners* ***believe*** *they are being responsible.*

Hunting ***is*** *a natural instinct for cats.*

2 Write appropriate endings for these sentences. Be sure to use the simple present tense.

a A bell on a cat's collar ___.

b Native birds ___.

c At night cats ___.

d Responsible pet owners ___.

e I always ___.

Writers use evaluative language to show what they think about the topic and persuade the reader.

e.g. *Attaching a bell is* ***better than doing nothing****.*

Responsible pet ownership is ***a positive step*** *in the protection of wildlife.*

3 **Circle the word to complete the sentence and show what you think.**

a It is (important / unnecessary) to know where your cat is at night.

b Watching television all day is a (worthwhile / foolish) activity.

c Mathematics is my (favourite / least favourite) subject at school.

d People (should always / don't have to) be kind to each other.

e Going on a roller coaster is very (exciting / frightening).

4 **Complete these sentences with a contrasting idea. Don't forget to use a connecting word if necessary.**

a Although many native birds have been preyed upon by cats __________________

____

b Many people enjoy going to the cinemas on the weekend __________________

____

c While nutritionists advise us about eating a healthy diet __________________

____

d I planned to arrive home early ____________________________

____

e Summers in Australia are very hot ____________________________

____

5 **The words below are notes made for writing an exposition. Use the words to write sentences. Make sure your sentences make sense. If possible use evaluative language to show your opinion and persuade your readers. Then write one more sentence to complete the exposition.**

Why Pet Cats are Important

a everyone cat cute cuddly

____

b help relax sit on lap purr

____

c always friendly never mean

____

d easy look after good friends no one else

____

e ____

____

6 **Complete the following sentences to show what you think.**

a I think it is important that ____

____

b I don't think it matters whether ____

____

c The most valuable thing for children to learn is ____

____

d It is ridiculous when ____

____

> Prepositions are placed in front of noun groups to show how, where and when.
> e.g. *Bells are fitted* ***in a secure manner***. (how)
> *Bells are fitted* ***to domestic cats***. (where)
> *A bell rings constantly* ***at every movement***. (when)

7 **Use prepositions and noun groups to tell where things are in the picture. Underline the prepositions.**

a The cat is ____.

b The bird is ____.

c The dog is ____.

d The man is ____.

e The child is ____.

8 Plural nouns are used for more than one. Rewrite these sentences using plural nouns. Be careful—you may also have to change the verb!

a The responsible pet owner made sure to keep his cat inside at night.

____

____

b The beautiful parrot perched silently in the highest branch of the tree.

____

____

c The child put the book on the table and sat down.

____

____

d The giant bullfrog was at the edge of the pond looking for food.

____

____

e The fairy danced along the beach and into the water.

____

____

9 These sentences are written in the past tense. Write them in the simple present tense to show what usually happens.

a The yachts raced from Sydney to Hobart.

The yachts ____________ from Sydney to Hobart.

b The boys ate their sandwiches on the beach.

The boys ____________ their sandwiches on the beach.

c The birds flew to the top of the trees.

The birds ___________ to the top of the trees.

d The girls spread peanut butter on their bread.

The girls ___________ peanut butter on their bread.

e The cat pounced at a ball of string.

The cat ___________ at a ball of string.

10 Proofreading

Where do the capital letters and full stops go? Mark them.

pet owners can help make sure their cats don't prey upon native birds they can keep their cats well fed and de-sex them to reduce the hunting instinct keeping cats inside at night may be the most effective step it guarantees the cats are not out hunting

Unit 6: Procedure

Procedures tell the steps needed to do something.

How to Make a Paper Folding Cat

Materials: 2 pieces of squared paper
pens
glue

Procedure

Stage 1: **The head**

1. Fold one piece of squared paper down along the diagonal to form a triangle.
2. Fold the new corners (points) down to meet the bottom corner of the triangle, forming a square.
3. Now fold those same points back up and outwards to form the ears.
4. Fold the bottom corner of the triangle up to form the chin.
5. Turn the head over and use the pens to draw in the cat's face.

Stage 2: **The body**

1. Crease the other piece of squared paper along the diagonal. Open it out again.
2. Fold the top edges in to meet along the diagonal crease.
3. Fold the bottom triangle back and glue it in place.

Stage 3: **Completing the cat**

1. Glue the cat's head in place.

Suggestion: Make a number of cats of different sizes. Create a background scene on a large piece of paper. Glue the cats in place.

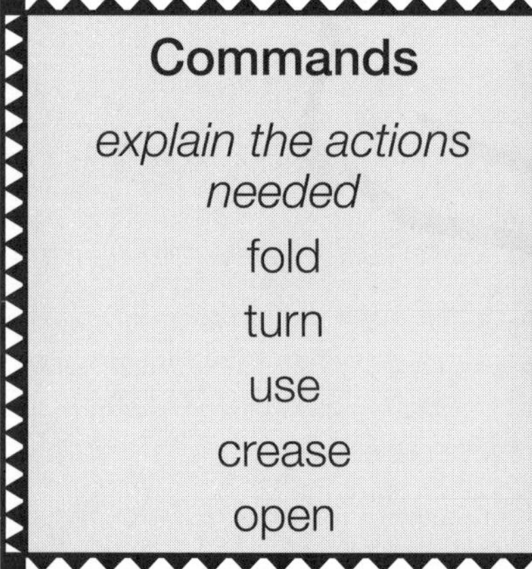

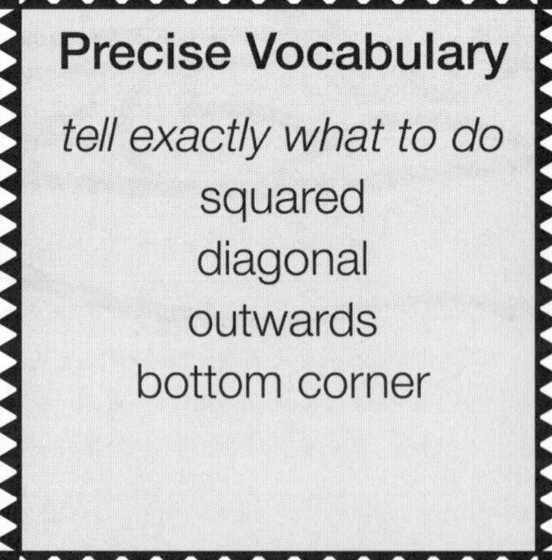

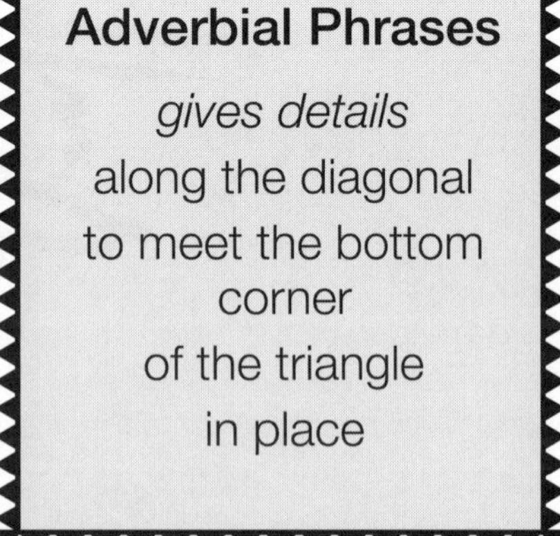

Did you notice these important things in the procedure above?
Read the instructions again and find any commands, precise vocabulary or adverbial phrases.

Answers

Unit 1: Narrative—Strike Me Pink!

1 Saying and thinking verbs
a We children were starting to ***complain***. (***whine***, ***moan***, ***grumble***)
b The adults were trying to stay calm and prevent us from hurting each other. (***remain patient***)
c Bending down Dad yelled "Strike me pink!" (***cried***, ***shouted***, ***barked***)

2 Nouns
a Because we lived near the ***seaside***, our cousins visited one Easter. (***ocean***, ***coast***, ***sea***)
b The ***grown-ups*** were trying to keep cool. (***parents***, ***oldies***)
c We hadn't been to the beach, but we did have a ***yarn*** to share. (***tale***, ***anecdote***)
d What ***laughter*** erupted at the sight of my father. (***hilarity***, ***delight***, ***merriment***)

3 Adjectives
the ***stony*** beach (***rocky***, ***golden***, ***beautiful***, ***safest***)
eight ***young*** children (***little***, ***nolsy***, ***well-behaved***, ***naughty***)
one ***terrible*** night (***dark***, ***stormy***)
on ***straw*** mattresses (***hard***, ***striped***, ***dirty***)
a ***happy*** smile (***pleasant***, ***quirky***, ***secret***)
a ***funny*** story (***true***, ***strange***, ***shared***)

4 Possessive Adjectives
a Because we lived near the beach, our cousins visited one Easter. ***we***, ***us***, ***my family***
b The dressing gown draped over his shoulders. ***Dad***, ***my father***
c Everyone's patience was wearing thin. ***everyone***, ***all the people***, ***the families***

5 Possessive Adjectives
a The young boy was very pleased to see his new boogie board.
b You need to apply sunscreen to your skin before going out into the sun.
c Our cousins came to visit us in their new car.

6 Direct Speech
a "I wish we could go outside and play," said Anne.
"You will be able to go out when it stops raining," replied Mum.
"But I don't think it will ever stop raining," sighed Jason, looking at the heavy grey clouds. "It's been raining for days and days."
b (Example)
"It will stop soon," said Mum, "but why don't you and Anne go and play a game while you're waiting."
"Yes, let's go and play a computer game," suggested Anne.

7 Picture Study
child, sandcastle, spade, seagull, crab, sand, rocks, sailboat, water, shells, sand
(Example)
a The ***child*** is building a sandcastle on the beach.
b The ***sailboat*** is sailing on the water.
c The ***rocks*** are at the edge of the water.
d The ***shells*** are lying on the sand.

8 Feelings
a At the beginning, the children were feeling ***bored/ unhappy*** because ***they couldn't go to the beach, they were whingeing and niggling at each other***.
b At the beginning, the adults were feeling ***cross/ impatient/annoyed*** because ***their patience was wearing thin, the children were fighting, they sent the children to bed early***.
c Dad was feeling ***surprised*** because we were all ***lying on the floor together, he said "Strike me pink!"***
d At the end, everyone was feeling ***happy/amused*** because ***everyone was smiling again, the sun was, out the cousins were going home***.

9 Picture Strip (Example)
As soon as the sun came out, Mark and Samantha decided to go to the park with Spike. They had been cooped up inside all day and now they were ready to play.
Samantha threw the ball high and Mark had to run backwards to catch it. "Watch out!" yelled Samantha when she saw Mark heading towards a big puddle.
Too late! Mark slipped over in the mud. "Good boy, Spike," said Mark, as Spike caught the ball in his mouth.
Mark was all wet and muddy so the children decided to go home. "Never mind," said Samantha. "We can come another day."

10 Proofreading
The children were inside the house. They were waiting for the sun to come out. They wanted to go outside and play. They were getting bored and were starting to fight. Their parents were beginning to feel annoyed. Soon the sun came out and they were able to go out and play. Then everyone was happy again.

Unit 2: Recount—The Day I Broke My Arm

1 Time words
One day ***after*** school, ***when*** it was very hot, we decided to go for a swim. The water felt cold ***at first*** but we were soon having fun and didn't notice it. Some friends came to visit ***while*** we were swimming. They came in for a swim too. ***After that*** we all got out and played on the grass.

2 Pronouns
a When Coach Kate looked at my arm ***she*** thought it was dislocated.
b My parents came to take me to the hospital because ***I*** was hurt.
c The doctor I saw was John Knox. ***He*** told me that my arm was broken.
d My parents were pleased that my coach had called ***them***.
e The doctor showed ***me*** how to keep my arm in a sling.

3 Adverbs
a I was running ***forwards*** to hit the ball. (***quickly***, ***slowly***, ***awkwardly***, ***sideways***)
b The coach ***quickly*** phoned my parents. (***soon***, ***instantly***)
c The coach came over ***slowly*** to see what happened. (***hurriedly***, ***anxiously***, ***casually***)

4 Adverbs
a The coach thought that my shoulder was ***possibly*** dislocated. (***certainly***, ***surely***, ***maybe***)
b We saw the doctor ***quite*** soon. (***very***, ***reasonably***)
c The fracture is ***very*** bad. (***quite***, ***terribly***, ***really***)

5 Adverbs
a My gym coach was ***quite*** helpful. (***very***, ***really***)
b The boy on the tricycle was moving ***very*** slowly. (***too***, ***really***)
c I could ***not*** wait for the holidays that started the next day. (***hardly***, ***scarcely***)

6 Sequencing Sentences
5 Samantha went next.
2 Before they left, they had to get all their gear together.
4 Bruce was first to have a turn.
3 Then they walked to the ramp.
6 Last of all Peter had a turn.
1 The children decided to go rollerblading at the ramp.
After that they all went home.

7 Exclamation Marks
I was lying on my bed thinking about what to do.
Suddenly— *rinnng*! It was the doorbell.
"Who could that be?" I wondered.
I rushed to the door and opened it.
"Surprise!" exclaimed Dad.
I couldn't see any surprise at first. I was puzzled. Then Dad brought something out from behind his back. A dog!
(Example) "Oh Dad," I said. "Isn't it cute! Just what I always wanted. Thank you!"

8 Story Writing—A Farm Holiday
a Jessie and Sam were going to their grandparents' farm for a holiday.
b They were very excited because they had never been on a holiday on their own before.
c On the first day they fed the chickens with grain and vegetable scraps, and collected the eggs.
d The following day they had a delicious picnic lunch on the riverbank and tried to catch guppies with a small empty jar.
e On the last day their grandfather took them for a ride around the horse paddock on the tractor.

9 Picture Strip (Example)
James woke up at 7 o'clock and quickly jumped out of bed. He was feeling very excited because it was a bright sunny day and he was going to the beach.
The first thing James did when he got to the beach was play on his boogie board in the water. He had so much fun catching the waves and riding them in to the beach.
Later that day James decided to go exploring on the rocks in search of tiny sea creatures. He did not find any sea cucumbers but there were a lot of little crabs scurrying about and tiny fish darting from here to there in the water. After a fun day at the beach James returned home happily. There were so many things to do at the beach he could go there again another day.

10 Proofreading
The children were visiting their grandparents for the holidays and they were really enjoying it. They had never been to Sydney before and everything looked so big and imposing. Suddenly they turned a corner and they saw the Harbour Bridge. Wow! The children had never seen such an enormous bridge before.

Unit 3: Information Report—The Didgeridoo

1 Relating Verbs
a A didgeridoo ***is*** used in traditional dances and ceremonies.
b Different colours of paint ***are*** used to decorate the outside of didgeridoos.
c The mouthpiece ***is*** at the narrow end of the didgeridoo.
d Termites ***are*** insects that eat mainly wood.
e Suitable trees ***are*** ones with hollow trunks.

2 Timeless Present Tense
a The Aboriginal people of Australia play didgeridoos to dance to.
b Small insects called termites eat the wood of trees.
c Traditional paintings are used to decorate didgeridoos.
d The didgeridoo player breathes in and out at the same time.
e Didgeridoos are played mostly by men.

3 Timeless Present Tense
Termites ***are*** insects that ***live*** in many parts of the world. Like all other insects, termites ***have*** three body parts and six legs. Although termites ***are*** often called 'white ants' they ***are*** not ants. Termites ***live*** in large colonies. Each colony ***has*** at least one king and queen. Only the king and queen termites ***have*** wings. Queen termites ***can*** lay more than 1000 eggs a day. Most termites ***eat*** wood, bark, leaves and other parts of trees.

4 Adjectives
traditional, ***musical***, ***Aboriginal***, ***living***, ***tree***, ***right***, ***difficult***, ***suitable***, ***desired***, ***narrow***, ***special***, ***continuous***

5 Adjectives
a The ***huge ferocious*** dinosaur stampeded across the field.
b The ***tiny annoying*** mosquito bit the weary traveller.
c The motorbike roared along the ***dusty narrow*** track.
d The fly was eaten by the ***large hungry*** frog.

6 The Simpson Desert
a The Simpson Desert is situated in central Australia.
b It is a sand ridge desert with red sand dunes running from north to south.
c The temperature can be hot during the day but cool at night.
d The Simpson Desert is an arid area with a rainfall of less than 250 mm annually.
e Many animals live in the Simpson Desert, including hundreds of birds, reptiles and mammals.

7 Using Commas
a Many different animals live in deserts including bandicoots, bilbies, euros, goannas, thorny devils and wedge-tailed eagles.
b When I go to the beach I always take my hat, t-shirt, sunscreen, boogie board, bucket and spade.
c There are five people in my family. They are Mum, Dad, Paul, Joanna and me.
d (Example) My favourite fruits are watermelon, strawberries, bananas, grapes and oranges.

8 Snakes and Ladders (Example)
The snakes and ladders game board is numbered from one to one hundred.
Players start the game at number one and finish when they reach one hundred.
The first player to reach one hundred is the winner.
Snakes and ladders are found at various places on the game board.
If a player lands on a snake's tail, they must move back down the snake and start again at the head.
If a player lands on the base of a ladder, they move up to the square at the top of the ladder.

9 Sentence Building (Examples)
a A ***paper plane*** is made from ***paper*** that has been ***folded***.
b The ***piano*** is played by ***striking keys with your fingers***.
c The ***telephone*** has been used for ***many years*** to ***communicate with others far away***.

10 Proofreading
Kelsey couldn't wait for the long summer holidays to begin. Her family was going on a four-wheel drive holiday to the Simpson Desert. Kelsey was looking forward to seeing the long red sand dunes, spinifex grass, wedge-tailed eagles, thorny devils and bilbies.

Review 1

1 Transforming Sentences (Example)
a The ***boats*** were going to the ***shore***.
The ***emus*** were going to the ***clearing***.
b The ***huge elephant*** was ***squirting*** the ***water***.
The ***old man*** was ***drinking*** the ***coffee***.
c The ***cat*** has ***short pointy*** ears and ***soft ginger*** fur.
The ***puppy*** has ***large floppy*** ears and ***short grey*** fur.

2 Expanding Sentences (Examples)
a The beaten-up stunt car went slowly down the dry and dusty road.

b The little girl happily wore a torn straw hat to the rocky beach.
c The sad and lost child sat alone on the hard wooden seat.
d The young bilby stayed motionless in the dark and silent burrow.

3 Sequencing a Recount
2 After they had gone a short way from shore, they dropped anchor and put their lines in the clear blue water.
5 Before anyone else could catch a fish, the skies darkened and a wind blew up.
1 The day was fine when the family set out in their motorboat for a day's fishing.
4 Then Paul felt a tug on his line but all he caught was a knotty eel.
3 Sam was the first to feel a tug on her line and she reeled in a beautiful bream.
(Example) ***Everyone reeled in their lines, and they headed home***.

4 Picture Study

	Nouns	Adjectives
a	forest	damp, dark
b	trees	tall, evergreen
c	vines	long, twisted
d	cassowary	graceful, old
e	wallaby	hungry, young
f	parrot	noisy, colourful
g	butterfly	delicate, beautiful
h	snake	dangerous, long

Sample Sentences (Examples)
a The damp dark forest had been there for thousands of years.
b The tall evergreen trees grew upwards towards the sunlight.
c The long twisted vines stretched from tree to tree.
d The graceful old cassowary explored the forest floor.
e The hungry young wallaby was looking for food.
f The noisy but colourful parrot perched high in the treetops.
g The delicate and beautiful butterfly sat motionless on a leaf.
h The long dangerous snake slithered silently through the leaves.

5 Punctuation
a "Look at that," said Mary.
"What is it?" asked Dan.
"It's a bilby," replied Mary.
b Ben and Jade were looking for tiny creatures in the backyard. Suddenly they heard a strange sound.
"Ssh!" whispered Ben. "Did you hear that?"
"Yes," replied Jade, also whispering. "What do you think it was?"
Then Jade tugged at Ben's arm. "Oh look!" she said, and she pointed into the lower branches of the flowering bottlebrush.
"Where?" asked Ben.
"There!" said Jade, watching the tiny birds cheeping for their food.
"Wow!" said Ben when he realised what Jade had seen.
c When I go to camp I need to take my sleeping bag, pillow, pyjamas, toothbrush, comb, two pairs of shoes and lots of warm clothes.
My favourite foods are spring rolls, fried rice, spaghetti bolognese, macaroni cheese and fruit salad.

Unit 4: Recount—Constructing a Worm Farm

1 Past tense
a lived
b told
c suggested
d organised
e spread

2 Adverbial Phrases
a ***On the weekend*** my grandma came to stay.
b We put in some bedding material and moistened it ***for the worms***.
c Grandma helped me set up a worm farm ***under the pergola*** in our backyard.

3 Plural Nouns
a many farms
b many blueberries
c many apples
d many dishes
e many fish
f many onions

4 Past Tense
a My grandma ***came*** to visit and she ***helped*** me make a worm farm.
b First we ***found*** a suitable location for our worm farm.
c We ***fed*** the worms nearly every day.
d The worms ***helped*** our garden to grow.

5 Adverbial Phrases
a During the school holidays my grandma came to stay ***for a week***.
b We went to the hardware store ***in the morning***.
c We went to the hardware store ***to get some worms***.
d We set up the worm farm ***in the backyard***.

6 Picture Study
a The tyre hung from the tree.
b The girl swung on the tyre.
c The boy threw the stick for the dog.
d The dog chased the stick around the park.

7 Writing a Recount—Coming to Australia (Examples)
a My great-great-grandfather came to Australia on a ship from England in 1864.
b He purchased a block of land to the west of Sydney and started farming.
c In 1870 he met Mary Cooper and they were married soon after.
d One year later their first child, my great-grandfather, was born.
e When they had four children my great-great-grandparents moved to Sydney so that the children could go to school.

8 Sequencing Sentences
4 Over the years they lovingly tended the tree and watched their children climb in it and play in its shade.
3 Then they watered the seed and waited for it to grow.
1 When the people moved into the house they decided to plant a tree.
5 One day during a violent storm, after all the children had grown up, the tree was struck by lightning.
2 First they chose the spot, dug the hole, and planted the seed.
(Example) ***The tree was so badly damaged that it had to be removed***.

9 More than One
The young ***children*** sat on ***their seats*** waiting for ***their fathers***. Today ***they*** were picking ***them*** up from school and taking ***them*** roller skating. The ***children*** already had ***their*** skates in ***their bags***. As soon as they saw ***their fathers they*** jumped up and ran to ***them***.

10 Proofreading
a My grandma went to the hardware store to buy some worms.
b We found a cool and shady spot under the back pergola.

Answers

c Last week we made the worm farm and gave it some food.
d We get worm liquid and castings to use on our garden.

Unit 5: Exposition—Should Pet Cats Wear Bells?

1 Connecting Words

a ***Although*** hunting is a natural instinct for cats, well-fed cats may be less likely to hunt.
b ***While*** cats like to hunt birds, birds do not like to be caught by cats.
c People think they are being responsible by fitting bells ***but*** bells are not really effective.
d A lot of people like to keep cats as pets ***but*** some don't.

2 Simple Present Tense (Examples)

a A bell on a cat's collar ***rings when the cat moves around***.
b Native birds ***are threatened by feral cats***.
c At night cats ***like to prowl around outside***.
d Responsible pet owners ***keep their pet cats inside at night***.
e I always ***brush my teeth before I go to bed at night***.

3 Evaluative Language (Suggested Answers)

a It is ***important*** to know where your cat is at night.
b Watching television all day is a ***foolish*** activity.
c Mathematics is my ***favourite*** subject at school.
d People ***should always*** be kind to each other.
e Going on a roller coaster is very ***exciting***.

4 Completing Sentences (Example)

a Although many native birds have been preyed upon by cats ***some people still do not care***.
b Many people enjoy going to the cinemas on the weekend ***but others stay at home***.
c While nutritionists advise us about eating a healthy diet, ***fast food is still very popular***.
d I planned to arrive home early ***but I didn't get there until late***.
e Summers in Australia are very hot but ***summers in England are not***.

5 Why Pet Cats are Important (Examples)

a Everyone should have a pet cat because they are cute and cuddly.
b Cats help people relax by sitting on their lap and purring.
c Cats are always friendly to their owners and are never mean.
d Cats are easy to look after and are good friends when there is no one else around.
e Cats are not expensive to feed and are easy to look after.

6 Evaluative Language (Examples)

a I think it is important that ***people wear seatbelts in cars***.
b I don't think it matters whether ***you have blue eyes, brown eyes or green eyes***.
c The most valuable thing for children to learn is to ***be kind to each other***.
d It is ridiculous when ***people cross the road without looking***.

7 Prepositions

a The cat is <u>under</u> the table.
b The bird is <u>in</u> the tree.
c The dog is <u>behind</u> a fence.
d The man is <u>on</u> the seat.
e The child is <u>beside</u> the swing.

8 Plural Nouns

a The responsible pet ***owners*** made sure to keep ***their cats*** inside at night.
b The beautiful ***parrots*** perched silently in the highest ***branches*** of the ***trees***.
c The ***children*** put the ***books*** on the ***tables*** and sat down.
d The giant ***bullfrogs*** were at the ***edges*** of the ***ponds*** looking for food.
e The ***fairies*** danced along the ***beaches*** and into the water.

9 Present Tense

a The yachts ***race*** from Sydney to Hobart.
b The boys ***eat*** their sandwiches on the beach.
c The birds ***fly*** to the top of the trees.
d The girls ***spread*** peanut butter on their bread.
e The cat ***pounces*** at a ball of string.

10 Proofreading

Pet owners can help make sure their cats don't prey upon native birds. They can keep their cats well-fed and de-sex them to reduce the hunting instinct. Keeping cats inside at night may be the most effective step. It guarantees the cats are not out hunting.

Unit 6: Procedure—How to Make a Paper Folding Cat

1 Commands

2 I folded the new corners (points) down to meet the bottom corner of the triangle, and formed a square.
3 I folded those same points back up and outwards and formed the ears.
4 I folded the bottom corner of the triangle up and formed the chin.
5 I turned the head over and used the pens to draw in the cat's face.

2 Writing Commands

a Walk to the door, turn off the light, and leave the room.
b Open your book to page 66 and write the date at the top of the page.
c Hop to the end of the path, do three star jumps and then sit down.
d Put the egg into the saucepan, cover it with cold water, then put it on the stove to boil.
e Fold your towel and put it into your backpack with your t-shirt.

3 Using Precise Vocabulary

a Write your name and date at the top of the piece of paper.
b Sit on the floor cross-legged and put your hands on your head.
c Stand on your left foot, hold your right foot with your right hand and put your left hand on your left hip.
d Write the numbers one to ten down the left-hand side of your page.
e Fold a piece of squared paper in half to form a rectangle.

4 Adverbial Phrases (Examples)

a Put the bottom sheet ***on the bed***.
b Tuck it in ***around the mattress***.
c Put the top sheet ***on the bed***.
d Tuck it in ***at the foot of the bed***.
e Fold back the top sheet ***away from the bed head***.
f Tuck in the top sheet ***at the sides of the mattress***.
g Put the pillow ***on the bed near the bed head***.
h Pull up the bedspread ***to cover the bed***.

5 Setting the Table

a Spread the tablecloth over the table.
b Place a knife and fork at each setting, with the knife on the right and fork on the left of each place.
c Place one plate at each setting between the knife and fork.
d Place a glass at each setting to the top right-hand side of the plate and above the knife.

Answers

6 Paint Blobs
Materials: a piece of white paper
three different colours of paint
scissors
glue
a piece of coloured paper

7 Creepy Crawly Puppet (Example)
Step One: Draw the head and body of an insect on a piece of card. Make it as big as you can.
Step Two: Cut out the insect.
Step Three: Cut the straw in half. Use sticky tape to attach the two pieces of straw to the insect's head. These are the antennae.
Step Four: Use the pens to decorate the head and body of the insect.
Step Five: Tape the paddlepop stick to the back of the insect. This is the handle for your puppet.

8 Pointing Adjectives (Examples)
a *That hat* is mine.
b Put *this cup* on the table.
c Throw *those balls* in the air.
d *That cat* has long silky fur.
e Eat *these chips* before they go stale.

9 Describing Adjectives (Examples)
a The *frightened horse* was galloping down the dusty track.
b The people stood on the beach looking at the *winning yacht*.
c The boy was surprised when he opened the *dusty box*.
d I found a *broken bottle* in the middle of the road.
e The girl turned around and saw a *horrible creature* coming towards her.

10 Proofreading
Scrambled Eggs
1 Break four eggs into a small bowl.
2 Add a tablespoon of milk and 1/2 teaspoon curry powder.
3 Whisk all of the ingredients together with a fork.
4 Heat a frying pan on the stove.
5 Melt 1 tablespoon of butter in the frying pan.
6 Add the eggs to the pan.
7 Stir gently until cooked through.

Review 2

1 Sentence Building (Examples)
a The *angry black* dog barked loudly at the *raggedy old* stranger.
b The *bright midday* sun shone on the *wide golden* beach.
c The *hungry feral* cat threatened the *little injured* bird.
d The *sad little* boy asked the *big friendly* woman for help.
e The *beautiful young* princess was frightened of the *ugly old* witch.

2 Jumbled Sentences
a The long black snake slithered silently through the dense grass.
b The hungry galahs squawked noisily in the tree tops.
c The young gymnast waited anxiously for her turn in the gymnastics championship.
d The pet cat stayed safely indoors by the fire all night.
e The pet shop was selling a litter of newborn kittens.

3 Plural Nouns
a The boys happily licked their lollies.
b The cats silently stalked the tiny finches.
c The peaches ripened on the trees in the orchards.
d The girls travelled to the zoo on ferries to see the monkeys.
e The patient farmers waited for the cows to arrive at the dairies.

4 My School Day—A Recount (Example)
School starts at nine o'clock. First of all the teacher calls the roll and we sing a song. Then we do maths until morning tea at 10.40. We go back in to class at 11.00 and then we do spelling and handwriting practise. Then we complete our language exercises until lunch time at 12.30. After we eat our lunch, we usually go out onto the oval to play. When the bell rings at 1.25, it is time for class again. We do different things in the afternoon but I like it best when we do art.

Unit 7: Explanation—The Red Crabs of Christmas Island

1 Time Connectives
a *Once a year* red crabs leave the forest and return to the sea to mate.
b The males arrive at the beach *first*.
c *When the females arrive* the males reach out and grab them.
d *After mating*, the males return to the forest.
e The females hide in the burrows *until it's time to lay their eggs*.

2 Doing Words Sentences (Examples)

a	return	I always return my library books on time.
b	watch	Many people watch sport on television.
c	arrive	There is usually someone there to meet visitors when they arrive at the airport.
d	join	Children join hands to form a circle.
e	lay	He lay on the grass and looked at the clouds.

3 Plural nouns
a crabs b signs c knives
d benches e larvae

4 Diagram

5 Homonyms
a The people looked out their windows to ***see*** the crabs on their way to the ***sea***.
b The people closed the doors to keep the crabs out of ***their*** houses.
c Scientists are ***sure*** that the tiny crabs return to ***shore*** after about a month.
d When the cyclist ***rode*** his bicycle down the ***road*** it was covered with thousands of red crabs.
e The ***two*** children watched the red crabs on their way ***to*** the beach and thought there were just ***too*** many.

6 Homonyms (Examples)

a 1 I can hop on my ***left*** foot more than fifty times.
  2 I ***left*** home at eight-thirty.

b 1 I like to ***watch*** television quiz shows.
  2 I use my ***watch*** to tell the time.

c 1 Leather is made from a cow's ***hide***.
  2 I like to play ***hide*** and go seek.

d 1 I like to have ***just*** a little bit of sugar on my cereal.
  2 The ***just*** king was fair to all the people.

e 1 It was the job of the lookout to ***spot*** whales.
  2 We have a favourite picnic ***spot*** at the park.

7 Spot the Errors

More than 50 million red ***crabs live*** on Christmas Island. ***These*** land crabs ***spend*** most of the year in the rainforest, but once a year ***they*** leave the rainforest and ***make their*** journey to the sea. The ***crabs*** can travel up to five kilometres a day. ***They invade*** people's homes and ***eat*** the plants in vegetable and flower gardens. They cover the roads like a moving carpet. When ***they*** arrive at the sea they ***mate*** and ***lay eggs*** before returning to the rainforest.

8 Crossword Clues

ACROSS
2 The males are the to arrive at the beach.
5 More than 50 red crabs inhabit the island.
6 Red crabs live most of the year in the .
7 Female red crabs lay over 100 000 .
8 Christmas Island is inhabited by red .

DOWN
1 Over 50 million red crabs live on Island.
3 Early in the wet the red crabs leave the forest.
4 Red crabs eat plants from the vegetable and gardens.

9 Prefixes and Suffixes

	Word	Prefix	Root Word	Suffix
a	inhabit	in	habit	
b	migration		migrate	tion
c	unheeded	un	heed	ed
d	return	re	turn	
e	ordinarily		ordinary	ly

10 Writing Sentences (Examples)

a migrate — The red crabs ***migrate*** from the forest to the sea each year. (verb)
b migration — The red crab ***migration*** begins early in the wet season. (noun)
c ordinary — It was just an ***ordinary*** day. (adjective)
d ordinarily — The crabs ***ordinarily*** leave the forest just before Christmas. (adverb)

Unit 8: Description—The Sydney Opera House

1 Noun Groups

a The Sydney Opera House is accepted ***as one of the world's greatest buildings***.
b The design won ***an international competition***.
c The project was completed by ***a team of Australian architects***.
d The ***massive complex*** can seat more than 6000 people.
e Be sure to include this landmark in ***your Sydney itinerary***.

2 Comparing Adjectives

Comparing Two	Comparing Three	Absolute
taller	most admired	full
more beautiful	most entertaining	unique
better	largest	empty
		first

3 Comparing Adjectives (Examples)

Comparing two
a The Sydney Opera House is more beautiful than any other building on the Harbour.
Comparing three
b Our sister always wants to have the largest drink.
Absolute
c The design for the Sydney Opera House came first in the competition.

4 Adjectival Phrases

a The Sydney Opera House is one of the greatest buildings of the 20th century.
b Its unique design with sail-shaped roofs is a popular tourist attraction.
c Visitors from all over the world have admired the building.
d The design, chosen from 233 entries, won the competition.
e Utzon resigned over a disagreement with the government.

5 Adjectival Phrases

a The Sydney Opera House is one of the most famous landmarks ***in the world***.
b Many people are greatly entertained by shows ***at the Sydney Opera House***.
c A lot of tourists ***from all over the world*** have been impressed by the Sydney Opera House.
d The building was completed by a team ***of Australian architects***.
e The Sydney Opera House, with seating ***for over 6000***, is on the shores of Sydney Harbour.

6 Writing Questions

a Where is the Sydney Opera House situated?
b Who designed the Sydney Opera House?
c When did work commence on the Sydney Opera House?
d How long did it take to complete the Sydney Opera House?
e How many people can be seated in the Sydney Opera House?

7 Compound Words

a overlap = over + lap
b seaside = sea + side
c surfboard = surf + board
d sunburn = sun + burn
e woodwork = wood + work

8 Clauses and Sentences

a x The design, ***which was chosen from 233 entries***, won an international competition.
b c The Sydney Opera House is a beautiful building and ***everyone should go to see it***.
c s The Sydney Symphony Orchestra is based at the Sydney Opera House.
d c Jørn Utzon resigned in 1966 and ***a team of Australian architects completed the project***.
e x The Sydney Opera House, ***which can seat more than 6000 people***, also contains a recording hall and rehearsal room.

9 Colons (Examples)

a There are many different ways of travelling to the Sydney Opera House: ***can bus, train and ferry***.
b A variety of materials are used in building houses: ***timber, bricks, concrete and tiles***.
c Many different animals are native to Australia: ***kangaroos, koalas, wombats, echidnas and numbats***.
d I enjoy eating many foods: ***hamburgers, sausages, potatoes, carrots and strawberries***.
e Visitors to the Opera House have come from all over the world: ***Britain, USA, Europe, New Zealand and Asia***.

10 Capital Letters
The Sydney Opera House was designed by Jørn Utzon. It is situated on the shores of Sydney Harbour right in the heart of Sydney. Visitors from Asia and Europe and many other places have visited Australia to see the Sydney Opera House. Many famous people like John Farnham have performed there.

Review 3

1 Compound Words

a	surfboard	It is fun to ride a surfboard on the waves.
b	clothesline	We always hang our washing on the clothesline to dry.
c	rainforest	Many different animals live in the rainforest.
d	postman	The postman delivers the letters every day.
e	catfish	I caught a catfish once when I went fishing.

2 Prefixes and Suffixes

	Word	Prefix	Root Word	Suffix
a	recognisable		recognise	able
b	greatest		great	est
c	visitor		visit	or
d	completion		complete	tion
e	international	inter	nation	al
f	competition		compete	tion
g	performance		perform	ance
h	innovative		innovate	ive
i	creative		create	ive
j	supervision		supervise	ion

3 The Sydney Harbour Bridge (Example)
The Sydney Harbour Bridge is perhaps Australia's most famous bridge. It links Sydney's northern and southern shores over Sydney Harbour. It is not far from the Opera House on the southern shore and Taronga Park Zoo on the northern shore.
At 1149 metres, the bridge is one of the longest single-span bridges in world. Its central arch is 503 metres long and 134 metres above sea level. There is a 52 metre clearance under the bridge for river traffic.
The bridge was designed by Sir Ralph Freeman and the design was selected by JJC Bradfield. The Bradfield Highway which crosses the bridge was named after him. After nine years of construction the bridge finally opened in 1932. It now carries eight lanes of traffic and has two footpaths and a double railway track. One of the most photographed landmarks in Australia, the Sydney Harbour Bridge is a 'must see' for tourists.

Unit 9: Biography—William Charles Wentworth

1 Compound Sentences
a Wentworth was educated in England but returned to Australia in 1810.
b Wentworth crossed the Blue Mountains and acquired some land.
c Wentworth opposed government by Britain and founded the Australian Patriotic Association.
d Wentworth helped establish the State school system and founded the University of Sydney.

2 Prefixes and Suffixes

	Base Word	New Word	Prefix	Suffix
	e.g. west	western		ern
a	explore	exploration		ation
b	contribute	contribution		tion
c	depend	independent	in	ent
d	turn	return		re
e	govern	government		ment

3 Writing Sentences (Examples)
a 1. It is fun to ***explore*** the rocks at the beach.
  2. Wentworth participated in the ***exploration*** of Australia.
b 1. It is rewarding to ***contribute*** ideas to discussions.
  2. Wentworth made an important ***contribution*** to the development of Australia.
c 1. We ***depend*** on air and water for life.
  2. As people grow older they like to become more ***independent***.
d 1. When you play games you must wait for your ***turn***.
  2. When you have enjoyed a holiday somewhere it is always good to ***return*** another time.
e 1. The Prime Minister is elected to ***govern*** the country.
  2. The ***government*** is made up of a lot of ministers.

4 Proper Nouns
Wentworth crossed the Blue Mountains in 1813 with Blaxland and Lawson. People could then travel to the western plains of New South Wales and many people settled there. Wentworth wrote many articles for the newspaper *The Australian* which he helped establish. He founded the Australian Patriotic Association to help Australia become independent of British government.

5 Capital Letters for Proper Nouns
Mary Williams
46 Kangaroo Street
Black Stump
New South Wales
Australia
Brownies

6 Gregory Blaxland (Examples)
a Gregory Blaxland was born in 1778 in the county of Kent, England.
b In 1806 he left England and came to Sydney with his brother John.
c After that he owned a farm at South Creek near the Blue Mountains.
d In 1813 Blaxland left his farm and crossed the Blue Mountains with Wentworth and Lawson.
e After crossing the Blue Mountains, Blaxland settled on a farm near Parramatta.
f He died in 1853.

7 Possessive Adjectives
a We must wear ***our*** hats when we go outside.
b They watched the show on ***their*** television set.
c Today it is ***her*** birthday and she is nine years old.
d You must wait until it is ***your*** turn.
e I'll never forget ***my*** first attempt at surfing. It was fun.

8 Adverbial Phrases
a Wentworth was educated ***in England***.
b Wentworth moved to Sydney ***with his family***.
c I went to the beach ***during the summer holidays***.
d The hungry children cried out ***for the food***.
e The Blue Mountains were crossed ***by Blaxland, Wentworth and Lawson***.

9 Prepositions
a The jetty is jutting into the sea.
b The boy is fishing on the jetty.
c The seagull is flying in the sky.
d The boat is under the jetty.
e The girl is standing beside the boy.

10 Writing Sentences
a William Wentworth was born in 1790.
b William Wentworth was born on Norfolk Island.
c William Wentworth came to Australia in 1810.
d William Wentworth came to Australia with his family.
e William Wentworth came to Australia by ship.

Answers

Unit 10: Information Report—The Giant Panda

1 Compound Words
- a farmlands
- b wildlife
- c somewhere
- d forepaws
- e sometimes

2 Writing Sentences (Examples)
- a Dorothy's farmlands were wide and open.
- b The zoo contained varied wildlife.
- c Jack had lost his pen somewhere.
- d The panda's forepaws were large.
- e Sometimes I eat chocolate ice cream.

3 Homonyms
- a The giant panda is easy ***to*** recognise with its black and white fur.
- b The giant panda belongs to the ***bear*** family.
- c Giant pandas can eat up to 3000 ***stalks*** of bamboo a day.
- d Pandas have a special thumb on ***their*** forepaws for gripping the bamboo.
- e Mother pandas usually give ***birth*** to one baby at a time.

4 Picture Study
- a Pandas eat the following things: bamboo, mice, insects, honey and eggs.
- b There are many types of bears: pandas, sun bears, brown bears and polar bears.
- c Many animals are native to China: pandas, elephants, deer, camels and tigers.

5 Complex Sentences
- a The giant panda, (which belongs to the bear family,) lives only in bamboo forests in China.
- b The panda, (which has become rare and endangered,) is used as the symbol for the World Wildlife Fund.
- c A special 'thumb, (which is on their forepaws,) helps them grip the bamboo tightly.

6 Combining Sentences
- a Adult pandas, which can weigh up to 150 kilograms, grow to about 1.5 metres in length.
- b Bamboo forests, which are home to giant panda bears, have been cleared to make way for farmlands.
- c Bamboo, which is an evergreen tree-like grass with woody stems, is the main foodstuff of pandas.

7 Relating Verbs
- a A baby panda ***is*** called a cub.
- b Bamboo stalks ***are*** the main food source for pandas.
- c Pandas ***are*** endangered.
- d A panda ***is*** used as the symbol for the World Wildlife Fund.
- e The head of a panda bear ***is*** large and round.

8 Present Tense and Past Tense

		Present	Past
a	The young panda lived with its mother until it was about 18 months old.		x
b	The panda spent most of the day eating bamboo shoots.		x
c	Pandas live in bamboo forests in China.	x	
d	Pandas have strong jaws and teeth.	x	
e	The giant panda climbed into the tree to sleep.		x

9 Collective Nouns
- a crowd
- b flock
- c bunch
- d team
- e mob

10 Adjectives	Sentences (Examples)
a giant	The giant turtle clambered up the beach.
b rare	The rare flower blossomed at night.
c endangered	The endangered numbat is rarely seen.
d baby	The baby koala stayed in its mother's pouch.

11 Synonyms (Examples)
- a Pandas have a 'thumb' to help them ***hold*** the bamboo.
- b Pandas usually live ***on their own***.
- c Pandas live with their mothers until they are ***approximately*** 18 months old.

Review 4 (Examples)

1 Noun Groups
- a ***A large flock of birds*** flew screeching into the treetops.
- b ***A long winding road*** leads to the top of the mountain.
- c The panda has become rare and endangered and is used as ***the symbol for the World Wildlife Fund***.
- d ***A panda's teeth and jaws*** are strong and powerful.

2 Synonyms and Adjectives
- a The ***brave young*** men ***travelled*** from Sydney to the Blue Mountains on horseback.
- b The ***huge white*** bird ***perched*** in the top of the tree and ***screeched*** noisily.
- c The entrance to the ***limestone*** cave was ***hidden*** by bushes.
- d William Wentworth ***founded*** the ***first colonial*** newspaper.
- e ***Many different*** birds ***live in*** the Blue Mountains area.

3 Adverbial Phrases
- a The people travelled ***to the Blue Mountains***.
- b The Blue Mountains were first crossed by Europeans ***in 1813***.
- c Pandas grip the bamboo ***with a special thumb***.
- d Sometimes pandas climb trees ***to sleep***.
- e Panda bears live only ***in bamboo forests in China***.

4 Complex Sentences
- a The tourists, who came from Sydney, travelled to the Blue Mountains by bus.
- b William Wentworth, who was one of the first Europeans to cross the Blue Mountains, was born on Norfolk Island.
- c The Blue Mountains, which are part of the Great Dividing range, rise to a height of 1097 metres above sea level.
- d William Wentworth was in favour of trial by jury which was introduced to local courts in 1830.

Commands and doing verbs tell the reader exactly what to do. The command is generally at the beginning of the sentence. It is understood that the command is meant for *you* to follow.

e.g. *Turn the head over* means that *you* should do it.

Commands are verbs in present tense.

1 **Read the procedure 'How to Make a Paper Folding Cat' and follow the instructions. The instructional commands are written in the present tense. After you complete each of the five steps for making the head, rewrite the steps in the past tense to tell what you did. The first one has been done for you.**

1. Fold one piece of squared paper down along the diagonal to form a triangle.
   I folded one piece of squared paper down along the diagonal and formed a triangle.

2. Fold the new corners (points) down to meet the bottom corner of the triangle, forming a square.

   ____

   ____

3. Now fold those same points back up and outwards to form the ears.

   ____

   ____

4. Fold the bottom corner of the triangle up to form the chin.

   ____

   ____

5. Turn the head over and use the pens to draw in the cat's face.

   ____

   ____

2 **The following sentences tell what was done. Write the commands that would have been given.**

a The boy walked to the door, turned off the light, and left the room.

____

b The girl opened her book to page 66 and wrote the date at the top of the page.

____

c The children hopped to the end of the path, did three star jumps and sat down.

d The boy put an egg into the saucepan, covered it with cold water and then put it on the stove to boil.

e The girl folded her towel and put it into her backpack with her t-shirt.

Precise vocabulary is necessary when explaining a procedure.

There is a lot of difference between *fold the square in half* and *fold the square along the diagonal to form a triangle*. Folding in half could mean forming a rectangle. This would not help make the cat. Sometimes illustrations add clarity to the written instructions.

3 Look at the following illustrations. Write a command to accompany each one. Be sure to use precise vocabulary.

a

b

c

d

e

A phrase is a group of words that has no verb.

In a procedure **adverbial phrases** give details about what to do. They tell how, when, where or why to perform the action. They often begin with a preposition.

e.g. *Fold one piece of squared paper* ***down along the diagonal***. (tells where)
Fold one piece of squared paper ***to form a triangle***. (tells how)

4 **Complete the procedure for making a bed. The adverbial phrases have been omitted. Make sure you write them.**

a Put the bottom sheet ______________________________.

b Tuck it in ______________________________.

c Put the top sheet ______________________________.

d Tuck it in ______________________________.

e Fold back the top sheet ______________________________.

f Tuck in the top sheet ______________________________.

g Put the pillow ______________________________.

h Pull up the bedspread ______________________________.

5 **The pictures show the steps to follow for a procedure. Write the instructions to accompany the pictures. Be sure to use commands, precise language and adverbial phrases where necessary.**

Setting the Table

a

b

c

d

a ______________________________

____

b ______________________________

____

c ____

____

d ____

____

6 **The following procedure does not provide a list of materials. Read the steps of the procedure and write a list of materials that are required to complete it.**

Paint Blobs

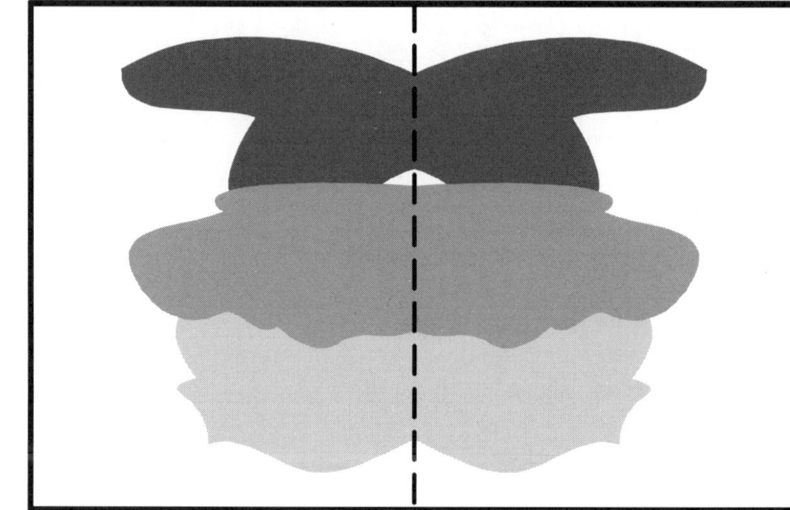

Materials: ____________

____

____

____

____

Procedure

Step One: Fold the piece of paper in half to form a rectangle. Open it out again.

Step Two: Place a blob of each of the three colours of paint on the fold line.

Step Three: Fold the paper in half again.
Carefully press down on the paper to spread the paint.

Step Four: Open the paper out again.
Look at the paint blob you have made. It is symmetrical at the fold.

Step Five: When the paint blob is dry, cut it out and paste it onto a piece of coloured paper.

7 **Write a procedure for using this list of materials. Be sure to use commands, precise vocabulary and adverbial phrases where necessary. Draw an illustration to show the completed item.** *(Hint: test your procedure to make sure it works.)*

Materials:

a drinking straw
a paddlepop stick
a piece of light card
scissors
sticky tape
pens

Procedure:
Step One: ____

> Adjectives describe or give more information about nouns. Pointing adjectives are used to point out just which noun is meant.
>
> e.g. *Fold **those** same points back up.*
> *Put **that** cat on the left.*
> *Place **this** book on the shelf.*

8 **Use a pointing adjective and a noun to complete each sentence.**

a ____________ ____________ is mine.

b Put ____________ ____________ on the table.

c Throw ____________ ____________ in the air.

d ____________ ____________ has long silky fur.

e Eat ____________ ____________ before they go stale.

9 **Describing adjectives give more information about nouns.**

e.g. ***squared*** *paper* ***diagonal*** *crease* ***bottom*** *triangle*

Complete these sentences using a noun and a describing adjective.

a The __________ __________ was galloping down the dusty track.

b The people stood on the beach looking at the __________ __________.

c The boy was surprised when he opened the __________ __________.

d I found a __________ __________ in the middle of the road.

e The girl turned around and saw a __________ __________coming towards her.

10 Proofreading

Write out the steps of this procedure. You will need to:

- ☆ **number each step.**
- ☆ **start each step on a new line.**
- ☆ **use capital letters and full stops in appropriate places.**

scrambled eggs

break four eggs into a small bowl add a tablespoon of milk and 1/2 teaspoon of curry powder whisk all of the ingredients together with a fork heat a frying pan on the stove melt 1 tablespoon of butter in the frying pan add the eggs to the pan stir gently until cooked through

Review 2

1 Sentence Building

Add adjectives to these sentences to make them more interesting.

a The __________ __________ dog barked loudly at the __________ __________ stranger.

b The __________ __________ sun shone on the __________ __________ beach.

c The __________ __________ cat threatened the __________ __________ bird.

d The __________ __________ boy asked the __________ __________ woman for help.

e The __________ __________ princess was frightened of the __________ __________ witch.

2 Jumbled Sentences

Unjumble the following sentences. Write them in the correct order.

a snake The through silently slithered dense black the grass. long

____

b squawked galahs in The the noisily tops. hungry tree

____

c waited her in gymnast for championship. anxiously the The gymnastics young turn

____

d night. indoors stayed The by safely cat fire pet all the

____

e was a of pet selling kittens. The newborn litter shop

____

3 Plural Nouns

The following sentences are written in the singular or about one thing. Rewrite the sentences, changing the nouns to plural. Be careful—you may need to change some verbs and pronouns too. Remember the rules for changing nouns to plural.

a The boy happily licked his lolly.

____

b The cat silently stalked the tiny finch.

____

c The peach ripened on the tree in the orchard.

____

d The girl travelled to the zoo on a ferry to see the monkey.

____

e The patient farmer waited for the cow to arrive at the dairy.

____

4 My School Day—A Recount

Write a recount of a typical school day for you. Don't forget to write in the past tense and use time words to connect the events.

____

____

____

____

____

____

____

____

____

____

____

Unit 7: Explanation

Explanations can tell how a natural phenomenon occurs.

The Red Crabs of Christmas Island

Christmas Island, a small island to the north of Western Australia, has a small human population, but a red crab population of more than 50 million. While these land crabs ordinarily inhabit the forest eating leaves and flowers and keeping the forest floor clear, once a year they return to the sea to mate and lay their eggs.

Early in the wet season, often just before Christmas, the mass migration begins. The roads are covered with crabs and signs, often unheeded, request that cars be left at home. People must close doors to keep the crabs out of their homes, and watch as crabs devour their vegetable and flower gardens, even the golfing green.

Red crabs may travel up to five kilometres a day. The males arrive at the beach first and hide in burrows, ready to grab a passing female when they arrive a few days later. After mating they return to the rainforest and the females take over the burrows until it's time to release their 100 000 eggs.

Crab larvae live at sea for about a month before returning to shore for the metamorphosis into tiny crabs. In four years time they too will join the mass migration, and return once more to the exact spot where they first came ashore.

Connectives

are used to sequence events

once a year
while
early
just before
first
after

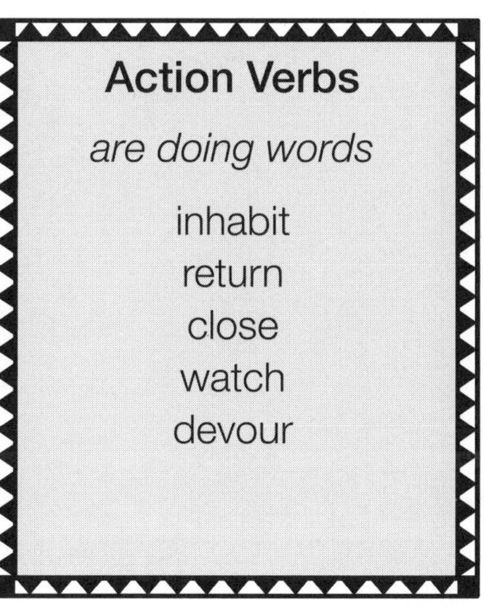

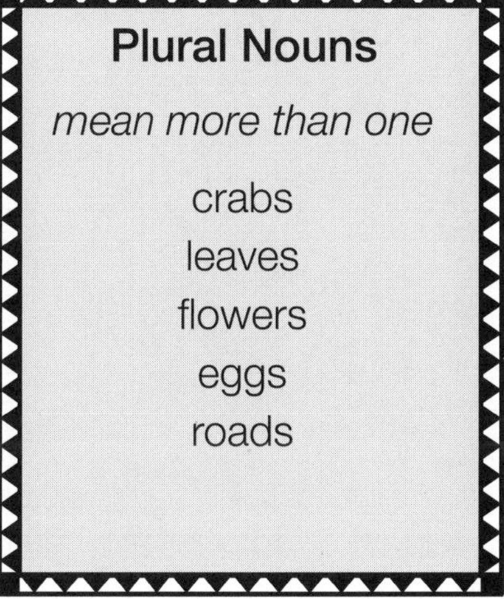

☆ ☆ ☆ ☆

Did you notice these important types of words in the explanation above? Read it again and find the connectives, verbs and plurals.

Connecting words are used to sequence the events in the explanation. Words like *once a year*, *after*, *first*, *before* and *until* help to explain the order in which events occur.

1 **Complete these sentences using time connectives and short phrases to explain the sequence of events.**

a red crabs leave the forest and return to the sea to mate.

b The males arrive at the beach .

c , the males reach out and grab them.

d the males return to the forest.

e The females hide in the burrows ______________________________

____

Action or doing verbs are used to show what is happening.
e.g. *The crabs* ***inhabit*** *the forest.*
The people ***close*** *their doors.*

2 **Find and list five doing words in the explanation. Use each word in a sentence of your own.**

Doing Words **Sentences**

a

____

b

____

c

____

d

____

e

____

Plural nouns are used for more than one.
Some words add *s*. e.g. *flower—flowers*
Some words add *es*. e.g. *beach—beaches*
Some words change *f* to *v* and add *es*. e.g. *leaf—leaves*
Sometimes the whole word changes. e.g. *person—people*

3 Write the plural form of the following nouns.

a crab

b sign

c knife

d bench

Read the explanation again to find the unusual plural form for the following word:

e larva

4 Diagrams can help add clarity to an explanation.

Draw a diagram to show the migration of the crabs from the rainforest to the sea. Label each place on your diagram and write phrases to show what happens along the way.

Homonyms are words which sound the same but have different meanings.
Sometimes they are spelt the same way, like *season* (a time of year) and *season* (to add flavour).
Sometimes they are spelt differently, like *their* (it belongs to them) and *there* (a place).

5 Write the correct homonym in the following sentences.

a The people looked out their windows to __________ the crabs on their way to the __________. (sea, see)

b The people closed the doors to keep the crabs out of __________ houses. (there, their)

c Scientists are __________ that the tiny crabs return to __________ after about a month. (sure, shore)

d When the cyclist __________ his bicycle down the __________ it was covered with thousands of red crabs. (road, rode)

e The __________ children watched the red crabs on their way __________ the beach and thought there were just __________ many. (to, too, two)

Some homonyms are spelt the same way but can have different meanings.
e.g. *I went to the pictures with my* ***mate*** *Jacob.*
Red crabs return to the sea to ***mate****.*

6 Write two sentences for each word, using a different meaning for the word in each sentence.

a left

1. ______________________________

2. ______________________________

b watch

1. ______________________________

2. ______________________________

c hide

1. ______________________________

2. ______________________________

d just

1. ______________________________

2. ______________________________

e spot

1. ______________________________

2. ______________________________

7 Spot the Errors

The following paragraph about crabs should have been written in the plural form. Some errors have been made. Read the paragraph carefully and underline any errors. Write the correct word in the space above. Remember to check the verbs and pronouns as well as nouns.

More than 50 million red crab lives on Christmas Island. This land crabs spends most of the year in the rainforest, but once a year it leave the rainforest and makes its journey to the sea.

The crab can travel up to five kilometres a day. It invades people's homes and eats the plants in vegetable and flower gardens. They cover the roads like a moving carpet.

When it arrive at the sea they mates and lays egg before returning to the rainforest.

8 Crossword Clues

Look at the answers on the crossword. Write a suitable clue for each one.

ACROSS

2. ______________________________

5. ______________________________

6. ____________________

7. ____________________

8. ____________________

DOWN

1. ____________________

3. ____________________

4. ____________________

Affixes—Prefixes and Suffixes

Affixes are units which are added to root words and change the word or meaning in some way. Prefixes are added to the beginning of words. Suffixes are added to the end of words.

e.g. *kilometres*—the prefix *kilo* changes the meaning from 'one metre' to 'one thousand metres'

population—the suffix *tion* changes the verb *populate* to the noun *population*

9 **Complete the table.**

Word	Prefix	Root Word	Suffix
a inhabit			
b migration			
c unheeded			
d return			
e ordinarily			

10 **Write one sentence with each word to show that you understand how the prefix or suffix changes the word.**

a migrate ____________________

____

b migration ____________________

____

c ordinary ____________________

____

d ordinarily ____________________

____

Unit 8: Description

Descriptions tell about the characteristic features of a particular thing.

The Sydney Opera House

The Sydney Opera House, on the shores of Sydney Harbour in the heart of Sydney, is one of Australia's most recognisable landmarks. Accepted as one of the world's greatest buildings of the 20th century, the unique design with sail-shaped roofs and overlapping shells has attracted visitors from all over the world since completion in 1973.

The design, chosen from 233 entries, won an international competition for its Danish architect, Jørn Utzon, in 1956. Work commenced in 1959 with Utzon in charge but under the supervision of the New South Wales government. The innovative design required new and creative approaches to engineering. Utzon resigned in 1966 over a disagreement with the government. After making some changes to Utzon's design, a team of Australian architects saw the project to its completion at a cost in excess of $100 million.

Despite its name, performances at the Opera House are not confined to opera. Many other functions are held there: concerts, ballet, drama, movies, exhibitions and conventions. The massive complex, which can seat more than 6000, also contains a recording hall and a rehearsal room. The Sydney Symphony Orchestra, The Australian Ballet, and The Australian Opera are all based at the Opera House.

The Sydney Opera House is a landmark to be included in any Sydney itinerary.

Nouns and Noun Groups

name the particular thing

Sydney Opera House

the heart of Sydney

landmarks

visitors

design

Comparative and Absolute Adjectives

compare one thing to others

most

greatest

unique

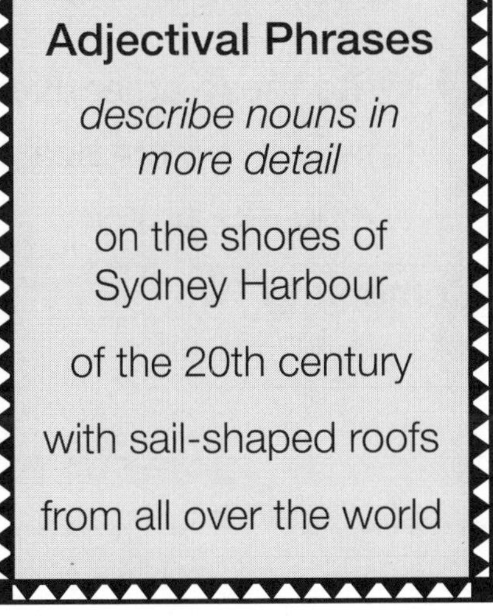

Adjectival Phrases

describe nouns in more detail

on the shores of Sydney Harbour

of the 20th century

with sail-shaped roofs

from all over the world

☆ ☆ ☆ ☆

Did you notice these important things in the description above?
Read it again and find nouns, comparative adjectives and adjectival phrases.

Nouns are the names of people, places and things. Noun groups may contain adjectives and other parts of speech.

e.g. *heart* is a noun
the heart of Sydney is a noun group

The Sydney Opera House	*is situated*	*in*	*the heart of Sydney.*
noun group	verb group	preposition	noun group

1 Write noun groups to complete the information from the description.

a The Sydney Opera House is accepted as ______________________________

______________________________.

b The design won ______________________________.

c The project was completed by ______________________________

______________________________.

d can seat more than 6000 people.

e Be sure to include this landmark in ______________________________.

Adjectives can be used to compare things. Sometimes *er* is added to a word to compare two things. Sometimes *est* is added to a word to compare three or more things.

e.g. *great* *great**er*** *great**est***

Sometimes *more* is used to compare two things and *most* is used to compare three or more things.

e.g *recognisable* ***more** recognisable* ***most** recognisable*

Some adjectives do not show any degree of comparison, they are absolute.

e.g If something is *unique*, it cannot be any more unique.

2 Write these adjectives in the correct columns.

taller more beautiful most entertaining empty first
unique largest better full most admired

Comparing Two	Comparing Three	Absolute

3 Choose one adjective from each of the above columns and use it in a sentence.

Comparing two

a ______________________________

____

Comparing three

b ______________________________

____

____

Absolute

c ______________________________

____

____

> A phrase is a group of words that has no verb. An adjectival phrase is a phrase that does the work of an adjective. Adjectives add meaning to nouns and pronouns.
>
> *on the shores of Sydney Harbour* is an adjectival phrase.
> It tells where the Opera House is.

4 Underline the adjectival phrases in the following sentences.

a The Sydney Opera House is one of the greatest buildings of the 20th century.

b Its unique design with sail-shaped roofs is a popular tourist attraction.

c Visitors from all over the world have admired the building.

d The design, chosen from 233 entries, won the competition.

e Utzon resigned over a disagreement with the government.

5 Write adjectival phrases to describe the nouns and complete these sentences. Remember: phrases have no verb.

a The Sydney Opera House is one of the most famous landmarks

______________________________ .

b Many people are greatly entertained by shows

______________________________ .

c A lot of tourists have been impressed by the Sydney Opera House.

d The building was completed by a team .

e The Sydney Opera House, with seating ,

, is on the shores of Sydney Harbour.

6 **Write appropriate questions for these answers taken from the text. Don't forget to use a question mark at the end of your question.**
Hint: many questions begin with *who, what, where, when, how, why*.

a *Question* ________________________________

Answer The Sydney Opera House is situated on the shores of Sydney Harbour.

b *Question* ________________________________

Answer Jørn Utzon designed the Sydney Opera House.

c *Question* ________________________________

Answer Work commenced on the Sydney Opera House in 1959.

d *Question* ________________________________

Answer The Sydney Opera House took 14 years to complete.

e *Question* ________________________________

Answer The Sydney Opera House can seat more than 6000 people.

Compound words are words that are made up of at least two separate words. Sometimes they are linked by a hyphen.

e.g. *landmarks* = *land* + *marks*
sail-shaped = *sail* + *shaped*

7 **Write the two words that make up each of these compound words.**

a overlap = __________ + __________

b seaside = __________ + __________

c surfboard = __________ + __________

d sunburn = __________ + __________

e woodwork = __________ + __________

Clauses and Sentences

A clause is a group of words which contains a verb and a subject.

A simple sentence has just one clause.
e.g. *The Sydney Opera House is in Australia.*

A compound sentence is made by joining two simple sentences together. Each one would make sense on its own.
e.g. *The Sydney Opera House is in Australia* and *it is very famous.*

A complex sentence is made up of two or more clauses, but one of them depends on the other one for meaning.
e.g. *The Sydney Opera House, which is in Australia, is very famous.*

8 **Read the following sentences. Mark simple sentences with *s*. Mark compound sentences with *c*. Mark complex sentences with *x*. Use different colours to underline the clauses in each sentence.**

a _____ The design, which was chosen from 233 entries, won an international competition.

b _____ The Sydney Opera House is a beautiful building and everyone should go to see it.

c _____ The Sydney Symphony Orchestra is based at the Sydney Opera House.

d _____ Jørn Utzon resigned in 1966 and a team of Australian architects completed the project.

e _____ The Sydney Opera House, which can seat more than 6000 people, also contains a recording hall and rehearsal room.

> Colons are used to show that more information is going to be given or explained: as in a list.
>
> e.g. *Many other functions are held at the Sydney Opera House: concerts, ballet, drama, movies, exhibitions and conventions.*
>
> Commas are used to separate each item in the list except for the last two items joined by *and*.

9 **Complete these sentences using a colon and a list. Remember to use commas in your list.**

a There are many different ways of travelling to the Sydney Opera House ____________

____.

b A variety of materials are used in building houses ____________

____.

c Many different animals are native to Australia ____________

____.

d I enjoy eating many foods ____________

____.

e Visitors to the Opera House have come from all over the world ____________

____.

Proper nouns are the special names for people, places and things. Proper nouns always start with capital letters.

e.g *Jørn Utzon* *Sydney* *Sydney Opera House*

10 **Which words need capital letters? Rewrite the passage putting in the capital letters. Don't forget the capital letters for sentence beginnings also.**

the sydney opera house was designed by jørn utzon. it is situated on the shores of sydney harbour right in the heart of sydney. visitors from asia and europe and many other places have visited australia to see the sydney opera house. many famous people like john farnham have performed there.

Review 3

1 Compound words are words that are made up of at least two separate words. Use the pictures to write compound words. Use each compound word in a sentence.

a  +  =

b  +  =

c  +  =

d  +  =

e  +  =

2 Complete the table. Remember prefixes are affixes which are added to the beginning of words. Suffixes are added to the end of words.

Word	Prefix	Root Word	Suffix
a recognisable			
b greatest			
c visitor			
d completion			
e international			
f competition			
g performance			
h innovative			
i creative			
j supervision			

3 Sydney Harbour Bridge

Use the illustration and the information to write a description of Sydney Harbour Bridge. Be sure to use noun groups, adjectives and adjectival phrases.

Notes

Australia's most famous bridge
one of longest single-span bridges in world
crosses Sydney Harbour
1149 metres long
52 metres clearance under bridge
opened in 1932
took nine years to build
eight lanes of road traffic
two footpaths
a double railway track
designed by Sir Ralph Freeman
not far from Opera House (south) and Taronga Park Zoo (north)
central arch—503 metres long, 134 metres above sea level
connects north shore of Sydney with south shore
JJC Bradfield selected design—Bradfield Highway—crosses bridge—named after

Biographies tell about the events of a person's life in sequence.

Unit 9: Biography

William Charles Wentworth

William Charles Wentworth may be best known for his part in crossing the Blue Mountains in 1813, opening up the western plains of New South Wales for further exploration and settlement. However, Wentworth's contribution went much further with involvement in the political and legal development of the State.

Wentworth was born on Norfolk Island in 1790 and moved with his family to Sydney in 1796. He was educated in England but returned to Australia in 1810. It was during this time in Australia that he participated in the historic crossing of the Blue Mountains and also acquired some land, before returning to England in 1816 to study law.

Upon his return to the colony in 1824, Wentworth helped establish the colony's first independent newspaper *The Australian*, where he publicised his political views. Wentworth opposed government by Britain, favouring self-government by the colony. In 1835 he founded the Australian Patriotic Association which drafted the constitution when self-government was granted in 1850. He also advocated trial by jury which was introduced to local courts in 1830.

Wentworth helped establish the State school system and founded the University of Sydney in 1852.

After influencing so greatly the way of life of the colony, Wentworth eventually returned to England where he died in 1872.

Compound Sentences

are two ideas joined by a conjunction

Wentworth was born on Norfolk Island **and** moved to Sydney.

Prefixes and Suffixes

are added to base words

western
settlement
contribution
return
independent

Proper Nouns

are used for special names of people or places

William Wentworth
Blue Mountains
Norfolk Island
England
Australia

Did you notice these important things in the biography above?
Read it again and find any compound sentences, prefixes or suffixes, and proper nouns.

Clauses and Sentences

A clause is a group of words which contains a verb and a subject.

A simple sentence has just one clause.

e.g. *Wentworth was born on Norfolk Island in 1790.*

A compound sentence is made by joining two simple sentences together. Each one would make sense on its own.

e.g. *Wentworth was born on Norfolk Island in 1790 and (he) moved with his family to Sydney in 1796.*

1 **Join the two sentences together to make one compound sentence.**

a Wentworth was educated in England. He returned to Australia in 1810.

____

____

b Wentworth crossed the Blue Mountains. Wentworth acquired some land.

____

____

____

c Wentworth opposed government by Britain. He founded the Australian Patriotic Association.

____

____

____

d Wentworth helped establish the State school system. He founded the University of Sydney.

____

____

____

Affixes—Prefixes and Suffixes

Affixes are units which are added to base words and change the word or meaning in some way. Prefixes are added to the beginning of words. Suffixes are added to the end of words.

2 **Complete the table using words from the Wentworth biography.**

	Base Word	New Word	Prefix	Suffix
e.g.	west	western		ern
a	explore			
b	contribute			
c		independent		
d	turn			
e		government		

3 **Write one sentence for each base word and new word in the table above to show that you understand how the base word has been changed by the prefix or suffix.**

a 1. explore ____________________

2. ____________________

b 1. contribute ____________________

2. ____________________

c 1. ____________________

2. independent ____________________

d 1. turn ____________________

2. ____________________

e 1. ____________________

2. government ____________________

Proper nouns are the special names for people, places and things. Proper nouns always start with capital letters.
e.g. *William Charles Wentworth* *Norfolk Island* *Patriotic Association*

4 **Underline the proper nouns in the following paragraph.**

Wentworth crossed the Blue Mountains in 1813 with Blaxland and Lawson. People could then travel to the western plains of New South Wales and many people settled there. Wentworth wrote many articles for the newspaper *The Australian* which he helped establish. He founded the Australian Patriotic Association to help Australia become independent of British government.

5 **Make sure all proper nouns begin with capital letters in the following address and information. Write your own name and address on the lines provided. Don't forget to use capital letters for proper nouns.**

Name:	mary williams
Street:	46 kangaroo street
Suburb/Town:	black stump
State:	new south wales
Country:	australia
Organisation:	brownies

A biography is an account of a person's life. The information must be factual. It is told in the past tense because the events have already happened. Time connectives are used to sequence the events.

6 **Use the skeleton outline to complete the biography. The main words are provided for you. To complete the biography you must write out each sentence in full so that it makes sense. Make sure you use the past tense and time connectives.**

Gregory Blaxland

a born 1778 county of Kent England

____

____

b 1806 left England Sydney with brother John

____

____

c owned farm South Creek near Blue Mountains

____

____

d 1813 left farm crossed Blue Mountains Wentworth, Lawson

____

____

e settled farm near Parramatta

____

____

f died 1853

____

> Possessive adjectives show who things belong to.
> e.g. *William Wentworth moved with **his** family to Sydney.*
> *Mary Williams took **her** books to school.*

7 Use the correct possessive adjectives in these sentences.

his her my our their your its

a We must wear hats when we go outside.

b They watched the show on television set.

c Today it is birthday and she is nine years old.

d You must wait until it is turn.

e I'll never forget first attempt at surfing. It was fun.

> Adverbial phrases give more meaning to verbs. They tell how, when, where or why the action takes place.
> e.g. *Wentworth was born **on Norfolk Island**.*
> ***on Norfolk Island*** tells **where** Wentworth was born.

8 Complete these sentences using adverbial phrases.

a Wentworth was educated ______________________ .

b Wentworth moved to Sydney ______________________ .

c I went to the beach ______________________ .

d The hungry children cried out ______________________ .

e The Blue Mountains were crossed ______________________ .

Prepositions are placed in front of noun groups to show where, when etc.
They are often used to begin adverbial phrases.

e.g. *Wentworth was born* ***on*** *Norfolk Island*.

on is the preposition used to begin the adverbial phrase.

9 **Use nouns to label each object in the picture.**
Write sentences with adverbial phrases to describe the position of each object.
Underline the preposition that begins each adverbial phrase.

a ______________________________

____

b ______________________________

____

c ______________________________

____

d ______________________________

____

e ______________________________

____

10 **Write answers to these questions using complete sentences. Your sentences will contain adverbial phrases. Underline the prepositions which begin each adverbial phrase.**

a When was William Wentworth born?

____

b Where was William Wentworth born?

____

c When did William Wentworth come to Australia?

____

d Who did William Wentworth come to Australia with?

____

e How did William Wentworth come to Australia?

____

Unit 10: Information Report

Information reports provide information about a particular topic.

The Giant Panda

The giant panda, which is easy to recognise by the black markings on its white fur, belongs to the bear family and lives only in bamboo forests in China. As many of the forests are now being cleared to make way for farmlands, the panda has become rare and endangered and is used as the symbol for the World Wildlife Fund.

Bamboo is the most important food of pandas. They can spend up to twelve hours a day eating over 3000 stalks of bamboo. Their teeth and jaws, which are used for cutting and crushing the hard bamboo, are strong and powerful. They even have a special 'thumb' on their forepaws to help them grip the bamboo tightly. Sometimes pandas eat other food: other plants, insects, small mammals and birds.

A mother panda usually gives birth to one baby at two-yearly intervals. She feeds the baby and looks after it until it is about 18 months old.

Adult pandas grow to about 1.5 metres in length and weigh up to 150 kg. They can live to be 20 years old in the wild. They usually live alone.

Pandas can climb trees and sometimes even sleep in trees. They do not make permanent homes like other bears may, and they do not hibernate. When it starts to get cold, they move to somewhere warmer.

Compound Words

are formed when two words are joined

wildlife
sometimes
somewhere
forepaws

Colons

introduce more information

other food: other plants, insects, small mammals and birds

Complex Sentences

have at least one dependent clause and one main clause

Their teeth and jaws, **which are used for cutting and crushing the hard bamboo**, are strong and powerful.

Did you notice these important things in the Information Report above? Read it again and find any compound words, colons and complex sentences.

Compound words are words that are made up of at least two separate words.

e.g. *wildlife* = *wild* + *life*

1 Match words in the first column with words in the second column to form compound words. Write the compound words on the lines.

a	farm	where
b	wild	paws
c	some	lands
d	fore	times
e	some	life

2 Write one sentence using each of the compound words from question 1.

a ______________________________

____

b ______________________________

____

c ______________________________

____

d ______________________________

____

e ______________________________

____

Homonyms are words which sound the same but have different meanings.

3 Write the correct homonym in the following sentences.

a The giant panda is easy recognise with its black and white fur. (to, too, two)

b The giant panda belongs to the family. (bare, bear)

c Giant pandas can eat up to 3000 of bamboo a day. (storks, stalks)

d Pandas have a special thumb on forepaws for gripping the bamboo. (their, there)

e Mother pandas usually give to one baby at a time. (birth, berth)

Colons are used to show that more information is going to be given or explained: as in a list.

e.g. *Sometimes pandas eat other food: other plants, insects, small mammals and birds.*

Commas are used to separate each item in the list except for the last two items joined by *and*.

4 Picture Study

Write a sentence using a colon and a list for each set of pictures.

a Things pandas eat

b Types of bears

c Animals that are native to China

A clause is a group of words which contains a verb and a subject.

A complex sentence is made up of two or more clauses, but one of them depends on the other one for meaning.

In the following sentences, the main clause is underlined and the dependent clause is written in *italics*. The verb in each clause is in **bold**.

Their teeth and jaws, *which* ***are*** *used for cutting and crushing the hard bamboo,* **are** strong and powerful.

The giant panda, *which* ***is*** *easy to recognise by the black markings on its white fur,* **belongs** to the bear family.

5 Complex Clauses

In the following sentences: underline the main clause, circle the dependent clause and put a box around the verb in each clause.

a The giant panda, which belongs to the bear family, lives only in bamboo forests in China.

b The panda, which has become rare and endangered, is used as the symbol for the World Wildlife Fund.

c A special 'thumb', which is on their forepaws, helps them grip the bamboo tightly.

6 Combine each pair of sentences to form one complex sentence.

a Adult pandas grow to about 1.5 metres in length. Adult pandas weigh up to 150 kg.

____

____

b Bamboo forests are home to giant panda bears. Bamboo forests have been cleared to make way for farmlands.

____

____

c Bamboo is the main foodstuff of pandas. Bamboo is an evergreen tree-like grass with woody stems.

____

____

Relating verbs are used to provide more information about a noun.

e.g. *The giant panda* ***is*** *easy to recognise by the black markings on its white fur.*

A panda's teeth and jaws ***are*** *strong and powerful.*

7 **Choose the correct relating verb to complete these sentences.**

a A baby panda called a cub. (is, are)

b Bamboo stalks the main food source for pandas. (is, are)

c Pandas endangered. (is, are)

d A panda used as the symbol for the World Wildlife Fund. (is, are)

e The head of a panda bear large and round. (is, are)

Timeless present tense is used to show what is usual or continuous.
e.g. *The giant panda **lives** only in the bamboo forests of China.*
Past tense is used for events which have already occurred.
e.g. *Much of the panda's habitat **was cleared** to make way for farmlands.*

8 **Place a cross in the box to show which tense is used in each sentence.**

		Present	Past
a	The young panda lived with its mother until it was about 18 months old.		
b	The panda spent most of the day eating bamboo shoots.		
c	Pandas live in bamboo forests in China.		
d	Pandas have strong jaws and teeth.		
e	The giant panda climbed into the tree to sleep.		

Collective nouns are names given to groups of persons or things.
e.g. *range* refers to a group of mountains.
birdlife refers to a variety of different birds.

9 **Use these collective nouns to label each of the pictures.**

mob bunch team crowd flock

a

b

c

d e

10 **Adjectives are words which give more information about nouns. Find four adjectives in the information report which describe or tell more about pandas. Use each word in a sentence to describe a different noun.**

	Adjectives	Sentences
a		
b		
c		
d		

Synonyms are words which have the same or very similar meaning to other words.

e.g. *Bamboo is the* ***most important*** *food of pandas.*

Main is a synonym of ***most important***.

11 **Build new sentences by replacing the words in bold with synonyms.**

a Pandas have a 'thumb' to help them **grip** the bamboo.

b Pandas usually live **alone**.

c Pandas live with their mothers until they are **about** 18 months old.

Review 4

1 **Add noun groups to complete these sentences.**

a flew screeching into the treetops.

b leads to the top of the mountain.

c The panda has become rare and endangered and is used as ______________________

____.

d are strong and powerful.

2 **Build new sentences by replacing the action word in dark type with a synonym and adding appropriate adjectives to describe the underlined nouns.**

a The <u>men</u> **went** from Sydney to the Blue Mountains on horseback.

____

____

b The <u>bird</u> **sat** in the top of the tree and **called** noisily.

____

____

c The entrance to the <u>cave</u> was **obscured** by bushes.

____

____

d William Wentworth **established** the <u>newspaper</u>.

____

____

e <u>Birds</u> **inhabit** the Blue Mountains area.

____

____

3 **Add adverbial phrases to these sentences to tell how, when, where or why the action occurs. Underline the preposition in your phrase.**

a The people travelled ____

____ . (where)

b The Blue Mountains were first crossed by Europeans ______________________

____. (when)

c Pandas grip the bamboo ______________________________________

____. (how)

d Sometimes pandas climb trees ________________________________

____. (why)

e Panda bears live only ______________________________________

____. (where)

4 Combine these pairs of sentences to form one complex sentence. Remember that a complex sentence has at least two clauses and each clause needs a verb.

a The tourists travelled to the Blue Mountains by bus. The tourists came from Sydney.

____

____

b William Wentworth was one of the first Europeans to cross the Blue Mountains. William Wentworth was born on Norfolk Island.

____

____

c The Blue Mountains rise to a height of 1097 metres above sea level. The Blue Mountains are part of the Great Dividing Range.

____

____

d William Wentworth was in favour of trial by jury. Trial by jury was introduced to local courts in 1830.

____

____